The Church has Lost Its Soul

We Christians Look Pretty Much Like Everybody Else

By Cal Seban

Cover Design by Aaron Muther

Acknowledgements

My deepest thanks and appreciation to my editor, Andrew Milam, without whom this book wouldn't be what it is. He read the manuscript. He struggled with it. He got it. And, he was spot on in saying what needed to be said, and offering suggestions for what were numerous improvements. Connecting with him was an unexpected treasure. His wife Marcia was an awesome copy reader, and another surprise blessing.

It adds significantly to the back and forth banter when your editor disagrees with the thesis of your religious views, and he is from your own faith tradition. It makes for some lively exchanges. Actually, it gets a bit testy. The notes in the margins of the manuscript are a treasure. He was not happy with how I structured the manuscript, as well as with what I wrote. If the subject wasn't so serious and important, it would have been really funny. I was still able to crack more than a few smiles and get more than a few laughs out of it. Even though he saw it differently, he did get it. And being from the same denomination resulted in his editing being even more valuable. If someone is a little perturbed with you, they tend to come down a little harder and be more critical than they otherwise might have been. In terms of the desired outcome, that is a good thing.

To my brother Rich, whose candor and honesty are a gift. What a blessing to have a brother who, while putting and reading the subtle undulations of the green, can engage in conversation about the meaning of life and the state of the church, still make the putt, and play to his 3 handicap. He, too, gets it. He understands. He serves. Fortunately for me, he also reads with the capacity to engage in a penetrating search for the essence, and the gift to know how to express it.

My thanks to Aaron Muther, who for the second time was gracious enough to share his creative gifts and expertise in formatting the cover, even when he was busy and didn't really have the time.

Above all, what a gift I have in a wife who goes out of her way to try to make everyone around her feel loved and special. She is a voracious reader and delightful story teller who lights up when sharing what she is currently reading. For some reason, though, that doesn't happen when she reads my stuff. But what she does share is so helpfully honest. She is so patient in sharing our retirement with the many hours I "retire" to my study. When I'm done, if I'm lucky, she won't suggest I come back up here and do some more writing. Her support is a gift to me every day. She knows how much this manuscript and its message mean to me. When we are too old to continue actively serving our Lord, what a delight it will be to sit in our chairs and read, to listen to the best story teller ever, and for me to look at the one whose eyes and smile won my heart, and whose graciousness, patience, and understanding have been a gift that I cherish.

Dedication

This book is dedicated to the faithful servants of our Lord who have responded to the assurances of grace and forgiveness in Christ with lives compassion, self-denial, and sacrifice. It is pure delight to have known so many of these "little Mother Teresas." I could mention a bunch of them, but they wouldn't know it anyway, because they have already gone to heaven, are about to, or are still so busy serving that they wouldn't notice. These folks have been my inspiration, and my reason for hope and trust in God's promises of a joy filled future.

The Church has Lost Its Soul
We Christians Look Pretty Much Like Everybody Else

Preface

I just came home from our local Circuit Pastor's Conference with my thoughts moving swiftly from one issue to another, and my emotions all over the place. This great group of pastors openly share their excitement about, and struggles with, finding models for ministry that speak to the culture. Millennials, for instance, might like some of what a congregation has on its website, and some of the ideas from the website of another. They might like the sermons of one pastor, and resonate to the daily devotions of another. Even our members follow the websites of other churches. They pick and choose, from here and there, fashioning their own belief system and lifestyle. If folks don't like what we are teaching, they move on. Recently, I learned about porches and decks, and the importance of getting to know your neighbors at block parties or a get-together on the patio. Today, it was impressed on me that our focus has to be quickly expanded to include a major emphasis on reaching Generation Z. The way we reach people, young and old, and the way in which we interact, has changed.

Our son just called. He and his wife asked if we could watch our grandson, nine year old Sam, while they attend our District's "Passionate Believers" conference, where the focus is on how we can more effectively reach out with the Gospel. The Gospel is pretty important to us. The Gospel is the "Good News" that we are forgiven and saved for all eternity through the suffering, death, and resurrection of Jesus Christ. The folks who attend really love the Lord and want to be the church. They want to be able to improve how we carry out the church's mission. We focus on the same objective at our District Pastor's Conferences and District Convention. We also have an annual, locally sponsored "Change or Die" Conference that addresses these same issues.

All of these efforts have been sabotaged, undermined, neutralized, and rendered ineffective. The shocking truth is that we have done this to ourselves. The framework and circumstances in which we carry out our well-intentioned efforts mitigate against the very outcomes for which we pray. My hope and prayer is to address the frustration and disappointment of sincere, dedicated servants in their desire to be faithful in helping to accomplish our mission. The world around us has changed, but we have changed too. We have forgotten the central core of the mission to which we have been called by Christ. The church has lost its soul.

People are struggling and searching for models of mission and outreach at a time when the church is experiencing significant decline. What I'm suggesting is that the way we have been going about it for the past century has become increasingly ineffective. In our efforts to reach out in a way that people are at least willing to listen to what we have to share, we keep trying to tweak and improve the current model or paradigm, not realizing that it is fatally flawed. We don't just need to improve it, we need to assimilate it into the larger, original mission of the church. This original mission has been contaminated and compromised. We have lost the passion and commitment of the original 12 disciples and all others in the early church who suffered persecution or were martyred.

We need to question widely held perceptions of the church and discipleship, shake the church to its foundation, and ask for consideration of a new paradigm that describes what is happening today. My prayer is that the journey will be an incredible experience, and at the end, we will find so much more of the peace that passes all understanding.

Several of my spiritual mentors were especially important along the way. R.J. Lillie, pastor at my home congregation, Ashburn Lutheran in Chicago, taught me what mission, ministry, service, and caring are all about. Rudy Reimer, campus pastor at University Lutheran Chapel in West Lafayette, Indiana, nurtured my understanding of what commitment and dedication is all about. Gerry Freudenberg, with whom I served as Associate Pastor at Trinity in Peoria, Illinois, taught me that "God is - to love." Dan Kelm and Jeff Dorth, both of whom I served with as Associate

Pastor at St. John's in West Bend, Wisconsin, started me down the path to understanding discipleship, discipling others, and what it means to be a discipleship church. This book explains how the biblical understanding of discipleship morphed into a whole different concept without the church even being aware of it.

During a recent visit, when our nine year old grandson Sam and I were talking about giving, I explained that when we make an offering in church, we are actually telling others about Jesus and helping others in His name. What Sam said in response blew me away. "Grandpa, it's better to help people than to get rich, isn't it?" Wow! He nailed it! He said it so clearly and so simply; this is the larger paradigm, the overarching framework into which our current paradigm for mission and ministry needs to be assimilated. Clearly, this was something he was taught at home by his parents. He said it in a way that anybody can understand. Now, all that has to be added as he grows older is the awareness that in our country almost all of us are rich.

The title, "The Church has Lost Its Soul," could be off-putting, to put it mildly. It's negative, depressing, somewhat offensive, and far enough out of the box to be considered sacrilegious. The whole idea of the church losing its soul is unthinkable. To even suggest it doesn't compute. I tried to find another title. What follows is the list of possibilities I came up with.

The Church in Denial
The Church has Compromised Its Mission
A Conspiracy of Mediocrity
Raising Support from, but not the Expectations of Our Members
It's not Just Sinners Who are Broken: the Church Itself is Broken
The Church's Alternate Reality, and I'm not Referring to Heaven
The Church found Guilty of Price-Fixing, Collusion, and Conspiracy
The Church in an "Altered" state
The Church's Altered State of Consciousness
LSD - Less Sacrificial Disciples
LSD - Less Selfless Disciples
How the Church Lost Its Soul Using Holy Smoke and Mirrors

None of them reflect the totality of what I see. None of them capture the essence of what the church is today. So I can't tone down the rhetoric. That wouldn't be honest or truthful. Some of the titles showed promise. They all contained elements of the big picture. They all reflect one dimension of the truth. However, when it came down to making the choice, all of them were attempts to nuance the hard truth in order to make it more palatable. All of the potential titles are attempts to sanitize, whitewash, or minimize what is a grave concern. Since the church is in peril, there can be no hedging and not a hint of being vague or ambiguous. The church has lost its soul and won't be getting it back.

My concerns need to be expressed in a straightforward, stand-up manner, characterized by transparency and authenticity, as well as understanding, empathy and love for my Lord and my brothers and sisters in the faith, all of whom were bought with a price. My hope and prayer is for all of God's created children to know the price Jesus paid for them on the cross and about the life of discipleship to which we have been called by the One who paid that price.

One of the toughest, yet most important, things to do is to be straight with a family member or friend who has strayed into behavior that is harmful to themselves and possibly to others. Friends don't let friends drive drunk. We take the keys away. We make it clear that they need to talk to someone. We may even take the bull by the horns and arrange an intervention. We do whatever is needed to try to get them to come to their senses. The Christian Church (in the United States) is intoxicated with an inflated sense of its own importance. This book is a wake-up call from a friend who also drank the Kool-Aid and didn't realize it.

I applaud those who are taking on the challenges that face the church by attending conferences that share best practices and models for congregational and denominational renewal. However, what these faithful servants are not aware of is that their good-faith and well-intentioned efforts, including training in situational evangelism, are built upon a collapsing foundation. This is the fatal flaw that sabotages and undermines our efforts.

Even after taking extra care not to come across as judgmental, critical, or blaming, one of my readers observed that at times I was judgmental and intended to get under peoples' skin. I responded, "No I wasn't, and, I don't." He responded with his gentle smile and piercing wisdom, "Yes you do!" Such is not my intent. All I want is for us to realize that in our walk with the Lord, there is more peace and joy out there than we have ever imagined. My hope and prayer is that by following the biblical path of discipleship, we will find it.

As for me, I am committed to using whatever time and energy I have left in mercy ministry, serving the lost, the last, the least, and the lonely. When physical rest is needed, I can't wait to study Hosea, Micah, and the Gospels again and to read the highly recommended books with related insights that were brought to my attention during the review process.

I recognize that we all come out of different theological traditions that have different theological emphases and use different theological languages and constructs. I found it difficult to detach myself from my own tradition and address this issue in a way that is inclusive, and I hope that my attachment to my own tradition and language will not be a barrier for others. All of my brothers and sisters in the Christian faith are so very special, a treasured blessing, and a source of tremendous encouragement. Earlier this summer, on two different occasions, several youth and adults from the local Baptist Church knocked on our door to invite "kids" of all ages to their intergenerational Vacation Bible School. They were all smiles and radiated joy and a love for the Lord. Their faith was an inspiration and witness to me. We're all in this together.

Writing this book took perseverance, and there were times when I was tempted to give up. Is it all worth it, since the probabilities are that only a few are going to read it? Sam was jumping from "lily-pad" to "lily-pad" in the leap frog pond at a water park. When he missed the next pad and fell in, he hopped right out and with a burst of excitement, enthusiasm, and anticipation, was ready to try again. The process of writing was a leap from pad to pad, and falling in the water more than a few times. On occasion, it would have been easier to give up, just stay there, and enjoy the warm water – the good life. I couldn't. There was yet another leap to make. What I see about the church has to be said. The pads that I had jumped on earlier in my life were all important in getting to where I am. Now there is yet another leap to be made. Suppose I don't quite make it? The leap itself will have been exhilarating. I wouldn't have given up trying for anything.

You're invited to try to jump to the next pad with me and join me in the prayer that it will stir the reflection and renewal needed to put forth our best effort in our calling to reach out with the Gospel to those who do not believe, and to serve those in need, in Jesus' name.

Chapter 1

An "Awakening"

Intended as Blessing, Experienced as Condemnation

These are exciting times for me. When you read what follows, you will wonder why. The image I have of the church, my church, is not just unfavorable, it is disheartening and brings an overwhelming sense of sadness. Most people would consider this circumstance to be a real downer. My excitement comes from knowing that before we can decide where we're going, we have to have a clear sense of where we are. I'm excited because I know exactly where I'm at now, which is a whole lot further down the road on my faith journey than I was just a short time ago.

I can testify to being a man with the kind of faith described in Hebrews 11:1 (RSV): "Now faith is the assurance of things hoped for, the conviction of things not seen." These are exciting times because I know who is going with me. Hebrews 13:5 says, "I will never leave you nor forsake you." Matthew 28:20 (RSV) reinforces the same truth: "And behold, I am with you always, to the end of the age." It took some time to get where I'm at. It will take others a while to get there too. When we do, we will find that it's a great place to be. Whatever else is happening, and whatever else we are experiencing, we will find the peace that passes all understanding.

This book is a hard read. As far as the whole church, I am saying that there is no hope for renewal. The church has failed to validate its proclamation of the "Good News" of salvation in Christ. The church has lost its way. The time when we could have had a major impact on our culture, and on the world, is past. I wish I could say that there's a future for the church, but time has passed us by. Our efforts, in terms of the larger mission of the whole church, are now an exercise in futility. If the battle is lost, what's the use? We come to a bitter conclusion. Why take the time to read it at all?

To some, it will seem like a message of blame, judgment, and condemnation. I can understand that reaction. I understand that one can come away with feelings of hopelessness and despair. It is a hard message. It is a heavy message. It is supposed to be, but it is not intended as criticism. I pray that, if it feels like it conveys an overwhelming sense of condemnation, we won't get discouraged, reject it out of hand, and give up before seeing it through to the end. Hear me out. It will be worth it. This is written as a wake-up call for the few who will be blessed to discover the fullness of joy and peace that accompany the life of sacrifice and service, and that follow from the assurance of grace, the free and undeserved gifts of forgiveness of sin and eternal life that come to us through the suffering, death, and resurrection of our Lord Jesus Christ.

While I don't hold out hope that the whole church will fully celebrate the "Good News" of the Gospel and be blessed by it, I pray that it will indeed be just that for at least some individual Christians, a few groups, and congregations. I pray that at least a few of us will find the blessing it is intended to be. In the end, there is a word of hope and promise in what would otherwise be a dark world. It is a hard read, but once we "get it," it is also very encouraging and uplifting, and we will be blessed abundantly on our spiritual journey.

The "Awakening"

It was an "awakening" all right, but not the one for which I was hoping. If it was an awakening in the spiritual sense of a new infusion of life, passion, and energy in the church, reminiscent of the "Great Awakening," the wave of evangelistic revival that spread across the American colonies from the mid-1720s to the mid-1740s, it would be exciting and cause for celebration. My awakening was of a different sort. I came to the startling awareness that the church is so very different from what I always understood it to be.

When it hits us and we see it, it blows us away. We realize that a very good friend, the church, and we are far out of the mainstream of life. How did it happen? How did it come to this? Our jaw drops as we realize that our good friend has led us astray. No, our good friend has betrayed us. We start to lose it. Our good friend and we have been going our separate ways for some time. We didn't realize it, and nobody told us.

My purpose is to be a voice that asks us to consider whether or not we are really being faithful to our calling as disciples. This is intended to be a reflective piece designed to help us look into the essence of our being. It is an opportunity to look deeply into our hearts and souls. Hopefully, it will serve as a catalyst for conversation that will help us reclaim and live out the biblical description of what it means to be a disciple, one who is called out by God to be a faithful follower of Christ. My prayer is that, in the end, we will find a greater measure of understanding, encouragement, renewal, and peace.

So here is what the book is all about. My intent is to explore the viability of a church that got caught up in the lifestyle of our culture, lost its way when it compromised, and thereby redefined the meaning of "discipleship." The result of its incomplete, understated, and therefore misleading and deceptive understanding of discipleship is that the church has given a less than inspiring witness. This, in turn, has led to the decline of a church that has lost its way, is no longer effectively carrying out its mission, and has become insignificant and irrelevant. During the process of redefining discipleship, the church has lost its soul.

I am writing because my passion in life is for the temporal well-being of the abandoned, the suffering, the destitute, and for the eternal well-being of all who do not know Christ as their Savior. In order to pursue my passion and reason for being, it is important to bring to light how we, as the church, have become a stumbling block to the Gospel doing its thing in meeting both our temporal and eternal needs. If we didn't know better, we would think that the church has been complicit in a conspiracy to perpetuate mediocrity.

Where Have We Been?

After serving for 50 years in ministry, one would think I would have a good idea of what it's all about – sharing the glorious message of the Gospel in preaching, teaching, and pastoral care, and inviting and encouraging my congregations to respond with lives of faithful service. I thought I understood the teachings of the Bible fairly well and have tried to be faithful in teaching biblical truth to others while living it out myself.

Then one day I realized I have been blocking, and in denial about, an important part of what God is saying in the Scriptures. It was quite a jolt. It knocks our socks off when we become aware that the church is quite different from what God called it to be. The church is now but a shadow of what it once was and a shadow of what it might have been. The church has lost its soul. Whoa! Where did that thought come from? I was stunned. How did I miss it? How could I miss it so badly? Where have I been? Have I been so caught up in the challenges I faced in the part of the church that was my ministry that I missed the big picture? Was I so wrapped up in what was happening in my own congregations, ministries, and denomination that I didn't step back and prayerfully reflect on the clues that something foundational was missing in the life of the church? Wow! I did miss it! I didn't get it!

My journey of coming to know Jesus as my Savior and my early life in the church left me struggling to play catch up when I began to study for the ministry at Concordia Senior College in Fort Wayne, Indiana, and then at Concordia Seminary in St. Louis. Most of my classmates had grown up in the church and knew a whole lot more doctrine and theology than I did. I didn't even have a good grasp of Bible stories or Bible history. Then life happened, and I continually felt like I was catching up. I married after my first year at the seminary, received a call to serve my first congregation, was blessed with children, had various ministry challenges on top of the challenges of the vocations of being husband and father, and was tracking tensions in our national church body. Then there was all the other stuff that goes on in life. I was immersed in what I was doing and just trying to be faithful. Through it all, I have been blessed beyond measure.

Then, all of a sudden, after being distracted and preoccupied for years, I realized that I had not yet put all of what was happening in my life as a Christian and a pastor into the larger framework of everything in life, most of which I wasn't aware. For various reasons, seeing the big picture just didn't happen. I thought I saw it, but I was clueless. All of a sudden, it came together and I saw everything differently. I never saw it coming!

Reflections from Our Kitchen Window

In the context of my ongoing prayer and reflection about what is happening in the church, this is what the world looked like to me Friday through Monday, December 10-13, 2016, nine years after retirement. It was a beautiful Sunday morning. Six inches of snow had fallen Thursday night. God's creation is awesome! For me, the beautiful blanket of white covering the ground is always a reminder of how, in forgiveness, the dirt and sin in our lives is covered by the white blanket of Christ's righteousness. "Though your sins be like scarlet, they shall be as white as snow; though they are red like crimson, they shall be like wool" (Isaiah 1:18).

The first thing I do every morning is sit down with a cup of coffee for devotions. The church was in the season of Advent, a season for remembering that Jesus came to save us from our sins, that He comes to us in the present in Word and sacrament, and that He will come again one day to take all believers to heaven with Him. My morning prayer was a "thank you" to God for having kept me safely through the night, a petition to keep me safe that day from sin and every evil, and a "thank you" that my wife's recent surgeries to remove cataracts in both eyes had been successful.

Since there was another snowstorm on Saturday night, thankfully, we didn't have to drive the twenty miles to worship at our congregation that Sunday. We had worshiped Saturday night because Makenna, our daughter-in-law's cousin, confessed the faith in which she was baptized, promising to walk faithfully with the Lord through the rest of her life. Instead, I read a chapter in Amos and made a few notes about Dr. Timothy Maschke's excellent book about the history of the Church: <u>Called To Be Holy in the World.</u> Dr. Maschke was a Professor of Theology at Concordia University, Wisconsin.

Next, it was time to read the Milwaukee Journal Sentinel, a morning ritual I look forward to. I noticed a piece on the op-ed page written in response to an op-ed piece in the previous Sunday's paper.

I must take issue with his mistaken belief that the United States is 'truly a Christian nation.' There is nothing in the U.S. Constitution regarding religion – Christian or otherwise – except in regard to freedom of religion as declared in the First Amendment. In fact, John Adams overtly stated that "the government of the United States is not, in any sense, founded on the Christian religion." And Thomas Jefferson, who took a quite dim view of religion altogether, observed, "I have examined all of the known superstitions of the world, and I do not find in our particular superstition of Christianity one redeeming feature. They are all alike founded in fables and mythology."[1]

That afternoon we were able to get to a vocal and instrumental concert by the extraordinarily talented young men and women at Living Word Lutheran High. My 75th birthday would be the next day, December 13. On the 13th, we also received word of the unexpected passing of my sister-in-law's brother at the age of 49. He was part of a group of ten of us that had recently vacationed together for a week. During that time, he was a powerful witness to me, as I was inspired, strengthened, and encouraged by his passion for the Lord and his faithful service in his community church.

I had scheduled shut-in calls on Tuesday. One, a faithful 92-year-old Lutheran School teacher who gave her all in a life of service, was now in hospice and about to be received into her eternal home in heaven. Another was a 91-year-old with serious short-term memory issues. Still another was already grieving the imminent loss of a daughter who had cancer. My wife was looking forward to the Lutheran Women's Missionary League Christmas Celebration on Tuesday.

The following Sunday, while sitting at the same window, I saw this article in the Journal Sentinel: <u>Where is religion headed in the U.S.?</u>

"For the first time in history, Congress passed a law that protects 'non-theists.' The Frank R. Wolf International Religious Freedom Act – named for a former congressman who championed freedom of conscience –is designed to shield all types of minority believers who suffer attacks and prejudice. It specifically says authorities must 'protect theistic and non-theistic beliefs as well as the right not to profess or practice any religion. [. . .] The first time inclusion of non-believers recognizes a transformation in U.S. society: the rapid growth of adults who say their religion is 'none.' A recent survey by the Public Religion Research Institute found that 'Nones' (those who claim no religious affiliation) have become America's largest faith category. They constitute 25% of the adult population, compared to 21% who are Catholic and 16% white evangelicals. [. . .] Rising secularism raises an intriguing question: Where is U.S. religion heading? Demographers and sociologists predict that faith will continue shrinking in America – but will remain more powerful than in other Western democracies."[2]

Seated at the kitchen table three months later on another Sunday afternoon, another article in the Sunday paper caught my eye.

Religion – About two Americans in five have confidence in organized religion, a steep drop from 1973, when about two out of three Americans felt that way. Three decades ago, only one in 10 adult Americans said they had no religious affiliation, according to the Pew Research Center; today, about a quarter of Americans feel that way. And one out of three millennials say they are "Nones."[3]

Where is God in all this? He's right here in the middle of it with us, in the midst of all of the pain, heartache, brokenness, and celebration. He doesn't promise that we will be spared sadness and sorrow, but He does indeed promise that He will make it all work for good. I want so very much for others to be able to know the same comfort and have the same peace that I have in Christ. I want all to know the hope and promise that are ours in Him.

Then it startled me again. I remembered that the church is quite different from what I always thought it was, and quite different from what God called it to be. The church has lost the very essence of what gives it life. The church has lost its soul. It is supposed to be so very much more than it is. It turns out that what we would expect the church to be, it isn't. My heart is heavy.

Thoughts about the reference to "religion" in the newspaper kept coming back. The contrast of world views and belief systems was striking. The church has always had its squabbles, but by God's grace and through the guidance of the Holy Spirit, we have always stumbled forward and found a way to maintain and preserve the core of Christian teaching. Even though our unresolved differences have resulted in a kaleidoscope of variation represented by hundreds of denominations and expressions of Christian belief, the church has survived.

The articles make it clear to all of us in the church that we are at a very different place in our relationship with the culture. We are no longer in the majority. Others have beliefs and views that are diametrically opposed to the bedrock of our beliefs. The word "spirituality" is an inclusive term that can refer to any religion and a variety of religious disciplines. While the world around us holds to the "Big Bang" theory and says that what we believe is a compilation of myth and legend, we need to remember that it is the Holy Spirit who brings us to faith in the mysteries of the Trinity and Jesus being both true God and true man, as well as in biblical account of creation. For Christians, the snowfall is a testimony to creation: we couldn't begin to decorate in the way a snowfall does.

Where is the Church in All This?

I spent many days meditating, reflecting, and praying about the state of the church. What is the most pressing need of the church today? What is it that the Lord wants me to do today? What came together goes something like this. For Christians, the world we live in and in which we serve and witness has passed us by. Our witness is less and less effective and the church continues to decline. Here in the U. S., we in the church have to recognize this new reality and take it seriously as we plan to move forward with our mission. Blaming the deterioration of the church on the changing ethics, morals, and values in our culture, and putting forth a valiant effort to have our beliefs codified into law just doesn't cut it. Actually, it will only create more bitterness and resentment.

"Hold on a minute. You said that blaming the declining morals in the culture for the deterioration of the church just won't cut it. What did you mean by that?" One of the threads that will run through this book is our lack of awareness of how we labor faithfully without an awareness of the big picture. While trying to accomplish our mission, we get in our own way and end up hastening the church's plunge toward disaster. We have undermined and sabotaged mission and outreach. "You can't be serious! We certainly wouldn't do that. You're going to have to explain that one to me." Well, I'm going to try.

So what's the plan? Great question! The plan is to contribute to a discussion that seeks to figure out how to move forward in our mission of communicating the love of God in Christ as we have come to know it. My premise is that there will not be another "Great Awakening," and that our efforts will result in minimal progress at best.

What will be written about us? Will it take chapters to write about us? Or, will we be given a short paragraph or perhaps just a footnote in the long history of the church? Will we be renewed in our desire to teach about the Kingdom of God as a dynamic entity that is always engaged and in action – the people of God living under the rule of God in lives of sacrificial service? We need to go out into the world described in the Journal Sentinel (the articles about the relationship between government and religion, and, religious affiliation in the U.S.) to seek and to save those who are lost, and to serve those who are suffering and in need as best we can.

The church isn't really respected anymore. We expect to find hope; we end up being disillusioned. We expect to find possibilities; what we find is disappointment. We expect to find joy; we end up being deeply saddened.

We begin with so much anticipation; we end up heartbroken. We want it to be even more than we thought it was; we realize that it's less. It can't even hold its own. We find that reality doesn't match perception. Whatever potential it had has been squandered.

Life is good for some of us, about 20 percent of the world's population. We are indeed blessed by the Lord to be able to enjoy the blooming of the flowers in spring, the warmth of the summer breezes, the rustling of the leaves in fall, and the snow-covered landscape of winter. We are blessed with family, friends, health care, shelter, food and drink, and all we need to support this body and life. At least 20 percent of us are.

But what about those who do not have enough of the physical nourishment that sustains us, little if any health care, and live with the reality of being powerless? We hear them crying out of the depths: "Where is God now? Where is Jesus? Where is my church? Who is there for me? I never thought my life would end up in a low-end group home for the aging where it is really hard to control the temperature, and where I get an hour visit from my family maybe twice a month. I never thought my life would end up like this! I just want to scream, 'Nobody cares!'"

Who is there for the refugee who was willing to risk his life and the lives of his family to escape the horrors of war, torture, or genocide? Who is there for those experiencing famine and for whom the death of family and friends is just a way life? Who is there for the disabled and mentally challenged? Where is God now? And where is the church? Wherever there are basic human needs like these, that's where our Lord wants to be present through His church. But all too often, the church is nowhere to be found, and people wonder whether God has forgotten them and abandoned them. How can this happen?

What we would have expected, isn't. What we would have been looking for, we don't find. What it should be, it isn't. All of sudden it hits us! All of a sudden we see it! All of a sudden we get it! As it begins to sink in, we try to sort it out. We begin to feel guilty that we missed it. Then we remember that we are forgiven! But we are still heartbroken because of what we have missed and what our life could have been. We are distraught.

We realized that others missed it too and that the church is nowhere near what it might have been.

Mystical is just not me. I'm your typical logical, orderly, linear, sequential, right-brained male. If there was a day that probably came as close to a mystical experience as anything that will even happen to me, it was the day I realized that the church in which I had been nurtured and which I came to cherish wasn't anything close to what it was called to be. I was having a difficult time getting my arms around an awareness that the church and life in the church were totally different from the description of life in the church that I was reading about in the Bible. How had the church missed the mark so badly? I had to reconsider much of what I had been taught and what life would be like from this point on.

I was scared to death and wildly ecstatic at the same time. While the church has tremendous potential as a community where we can find spiritual healing, it has become a very unhealthy place to be. What I saw was so very different from what God wanted it to be. The church that I knew and loved, and still do, has morphed into something that is nothing like it was intended to be. It has changed, and it doesn't seem as if anybody has noticed.

Had all the Bible classes I taught about the church and what it means to be a follower of Christ conveyed a distortion of biblical teaching? My church didn't look anything like the description I was reading about in the Bible. How had the church missed the boat by so much? What happened? How did it happen? When did it happen? It's like my eyes were opened and I saw the church in a whole new and different way. At the same time it was depressing, because I had a taste of what the church could be. What I saw was something very different than the understanding I had been living with all these years. A whole new level of awareness was washing over me, and it was about as close as this old boy would ever get to that mystical experience. All I knew was that I had to go back and prayerfully reflect on all I had been taught about this over the years. Where did my church go wrong?

It is numbing, both mentally and physically, when one day we realize that one of the pillars on which we have built the structure of our life is crumbling. We are saddened and disillusioned. It's like experiencing a death in the family with all of the feelings of grief, sadness, and loss that go along with it. The foundation of the church is still sound, but the structural integrity of the building has been compromised. The pillars are deteriorating. Core principles on which it was built are crumbling. It's not that we are defeated, but the wind has been taken out of our sails, and we are distressed to the point where we have difficulty functioning. Our core beliefs about life and reality are eroding. We realize that much of what we taught has glossed over some of the essentials. How did I miss it? How did others miss it? What happened? Where did we go wrong? How did we miss it so badly?

Spring Came One Foggy Morning

When warm air blows over the snow, the fog follows close behind. Almost everything is seen differently. Most of us in the church have missed out on so much of what it means to live life to the fullest. Somehow we have become distracted. Somehow we lost our direction and focus – we lost our way. The people I have served have missed out on the fullness of joy. Most have not experienced all of the celebration and expectation that is there to claim. Most of them have missed out on the feeling of fulfillment that comes with living a life of sacrificial service.

My world really has been turned upside down. I can't quite come to terms with the new reality. I have to pray and think these things through and see if I can make some sense of it all, and then, with the help of the Holy Spirit, figure out what I am going to do about it. Am I going to have to remake my whole life?

Sitting at our kitchen table and looking out at our back yard is a beautiful sight anytime. It was especially striking early one late spring morning. The sun was starting to shine on the flowers in our back gardens. They were planted a little earlier than usual because my wife just had a knee replaced, and I wanted her to be able to enjoy them during her recovery. Along with the flowers came the spring migration of the birds. We have lots of birds common to our area, including robins, goldfinches, cardinals, and house-finches. During the spring migration we also have purple finches, evening grosbeaks, Baltimore orioles and a few indigo buntings. These are special moments of enjoying God's creation.

During what could have been a glorious moment delighting in and celebrating God's creation, dark clouds of deep sadness overwhelmed me. I was disconsolate. Over the past several months, I had come to the awareness that the world as I knew it was coming apart. The church was no longer what I thought it was for most of my life. On one level I realized it; on another level I couldn't accept it. What I had held in such high regard – the institutional church – had so totally let me down, had so totally disappointed me, and had so totally failed me and so many others. But I was part of its failure. I am just as culpable as everyone else. I was experiencing an almost overwhelming sense of disappointment, loss, and sadness.

On that spring morning, I was overcome with emotion that had been building for months. My vision of the church was in shambles. It wasn't the church I revered. In the lives of individuals and congregations, there are some inspirational and encouraging examples of love, faith, and sacrificial service; however, the big picture didn't reflect the magnificent entity that I had understood it to be. It wasn't even close. Actually, it was perilously close to being a fraud. The organizing principles of my life were shaken to their foundation and would have to be reordered.

We're not just talking about nuances of difference within the household of faith. We're not talking about the doctrinal or theological squabbles, the usual in-house, denominational conflicts. We in the church have abandoned a core element in our charge to love the Lord our God with all our heart, soul and mind, and love our neighbor as ourselves. This trend reaches across all denominational lines and expressions of Christianity. What I realized was missing could only be found in a few small corners of the church. What happened?

The morning regained most of its beauty and splendor; the creation was magnificent, but I was still trying to shake some lingering clouds. Praying for strength, I was finally just letting go. I was no longer blocking, repressing, or distorting the truth. I was no longer denying reality. Now I could begin to come to terms with it, not just try to survive. Now I could pray about all of this in a different way. Now that I had come to terms with it, I could begin to share what I was seeing with others. I don't know where this is all going or where it will lead. What's certain is that it is a road that has to be traveled. There is no going back. I was confident about what I saw and I wasn't. I was at peace, and I wasn't. But it was a glorious morning, fresh, beautiful, and full of promise.

Coffee, Cussin,' and Cigarettes

Looking out the same window a few days later on a drizzly morning, the splendor of the lilacs had faded, ending a longer than usual display of one of the most beautiful blooms we have enjoyed in the thirty-two years we have lived here. Their beauty had been an extended testimony to the glory of the creation and the Creator for almost three weeks. I stuffed the Journal Sentinel into my briefcase and headed for McDonald's - Cal's Study West.

While enjoying a cup of coffee and a sausage biscuit, I was distracted more than usual by what was going on around me. What first caught my attention was an old timer using "f" bombs loud enough for the dozen or so of us around him to be able to hear; thankfully, there were no children there at the time. A steady line of cars passed through the drive thru next to my window, and I wondered where each of them was going and what their day would be like. Out in the parking lot a young woman took her time smoking a cigarette. Clearly she enjoyed the brief sense of calm and peace it gave her in the midst of what it was that made her anxious.

Moving on to the morning paper, and what was happening in the world around us, the front page covered the story of the merciless, horrendous, and heartbreaking terrorist bombing at an Ariana Grande concert in

Manchester, England, where 22 people were killed and another 139 wounded, more than half of them children. Most of Grande's fans were young girls. What role does a distorted and twisted interpretation of religion have in the radicalizing of those who are duped, manipulated, and used as pawns? How does this happen? Somewhere along the path of their life, they experienced enough emotional pain that they are able to twist, warp, and distort something they experience as sacred into an evil hatred that justifies killing and maiming to further what they consider to be a righteous cause.

Other lead stories included President Trump's official visits to Saudi Arabia, Jerusalem, and Rome, Russian influence on our recent presidential election, and the special prosecutor. Then, there was a sampling of stories about the wealth gap, satisfying the demands of boards of directors for a tax code that would bring an increased return on investment, funding Social Security, Medicare and Medicaid, trade policy, and environmental concerns. In all of this, news about the church was nowhere to be found. I went back to my coffee, trying again to come to terms with this new awareness that the church has lost its soul and what that means in the midst of all that is going on in the world.

The clergy are aware of the spiritual challenge of using the Word to teach and inspire their members to be on fire for the Lord. Pastors are aware that the level of commitment of most members is significantly lower than they pray for. When it comes to faith, people have their "comfort zone" and don't like it when they are challenged to the point where they start to get anxious. They don't want to be inconvenienced. They have their own goals, hopes, and dreams and want a church with expectations that fit neatly into what they want in their religion. We pastors are all aware of this. It's our biggest challenge.

What went right past me was the cumulative effect of this mindset on the whole church. The preferred religion that our members create for themselves drains the church spiritually. We are exhausted and broken. The church doesn't have much left and hasn't for some time. Our tanks are so empty that we can hardly function. There is no energy. There is no enthusiasm. We just muddle along. We just go through the motions. We offer very little for our members to really get excited about.

For years, I focused on Bible study and the important doctrines taught in Luther's Small Catechism. I let our members down by not being much more specific about what mature Christians look like, how they establish their priorities, and how to walk in the footsteps of Christ. They learned only half of what spiritual maturity was all about. At the same time, I was oblivious to how the cumulative effect of this spiritual epidemic that I had helped to perpetuate had negatively impacted the whole church. We hardly resemble the early church. We do not begin to share the joy of the twelve Apostles and the other disciples from New Testament times. The church that I had held in such high regard had bailed on carrying out half of its mission. I was devastated.

Then, relatively recently, the true picture of what it meant to be the church began to come together. Out of all that I had lived and learned, there emerged a framework of understanding into which all the pieces fit. It was like a dimmer rather than a light switch, gradually, little by little, the light shone brightly and revealed the outlines of the whole structure. It was like dialing in the focus on a zoom lens. Now, the picture is clear. It all came together as a working model.

A Letter to My Brothers and Sisters in the Family of Faith

While we have our differences in doctrine and ethics resulting from the application of different approaches to biblical interpretation, I believe what I have to say applies to the whole church and crosses denominational lines. It speaks to all who hold to the core teachings that have defined Christians since the first century. The first is the belief in the Holy Trinity, the mystery that there are three persons and yet only one God. The second foundational belief is the mystery that Jesus is both true God and true man. He is true man so that He could actually experience and suffer the pain and agony of the punishment our sins deserve. He is true God so that His suffering would be sufficient to atone for the sins of every person who ever lived. He came into this world and suffered and died on a cross for our sins and rose again on Easter morning as the victor over sin, death, and the devil. Believers share in His victory! They have the assurance of forgiveness and the certainty of eternal life in heaven. These two beliefs are the bedrock foundation of all who call themselves Christians.

The church is the community of those who, through the work of the Holy Spirit, have been called and brought to faith in our Savior Jesus Christ, through whom we receive forgiveness and eternal life as a free and undeserved gifts. This is what we Christians call the Gospel or the "Good News," summed up in John 3:16: "For God so loved the world, that he gave his only Son, that whoever believes in him should not perish but have eternal life." The church is a believing community of disciples, called to share this wonderful news and to live lives of sacrifice and service. The common denominator of what all Christians believe is set forth in the three ancient creeds of the church: the Apostles, the Nicene, and the Athanasian.

My reflections in this book are written in love and with the deep and sincere concern of a Christian to all of my brothers and sisters in the faith. Where we go from here remains to be seen. Yet, we know God always has a plan, and it is always intended to work out for our good and His glory. Romans 11:33, 34 (NIV) says, "Oh, the depth of the riches of the wisdom and knowledge of God! How unsearchable are his judgment, and his paths beyond tracing out! "Who has known the mind of the Lord? Or who has been his counselor?" Isaiah 55:8-10 (NIV) reads, "'For my thoughts are not your thoughts, neither are your ways my ways,' declares the Lord. 'As the heavens are higher than the earth, so are my ways higher than your ways and my thoughts than your thoughts.'" Romans 8:28 (NIV) teaches, "And we know that in all things God works for the good of those who love him, who have been called according to his purpose." God always has His reasons, and they all reflect His desire to bring blessing.

Why Go On?

Where will the journey of the church in history go from here? The hopeful, positive, and optimistic part of me wants the glass to be half full and for our "better angels" to prevail. The part of me that has to be forthright, transparent, and realistic compels me to conclude the glass is almost empty and our "better angels" will not win out. I don't expect much of anything to change. I really don't expect this book to make more than a tiny difference. So why do it? Why continue with the task? The church has already lost its soul.

We are God's own people called out of darkness into His marvelous light; this is good! But we see ourselves as privileged characters; this is bad! We are just like the Old Testament people of God who felt they had some special status because they were children of Abraham. Look what happened to them; their land was conquered, and they were taken into exile in Assyria and Babylonia. This was followed by God's promise of deliverance, which came in the person of Christ. I'm certainly not suggesting that the same sequence of events (unfaithfulness, military defeat, exile, promise, and deliverance) needs to or will happen again. We have been delivered through the sacrifice of God's own Son, the Messiah, and given a new beginning, a new community of faith, and a new church. That's already happened. I am suggesting that Jesus sees us the way He saw the Pharisees and Sadducees who reveled in their being God's chosen people, the children of Abraham. As John the Baptist said to them, "You brood of vipers! . . . Produce fruit in keeping with repentance. And do not think you can say to yourselves, 'We have Abraham as our father,' I tell you that out of these stones God can raise up children for Abraham" (Matthew 3:7-9, NIV). How much has each of us done this week to further the work of the Kingdom? Is our faith bearing abundant fruit?

If the church is not going to begin a process of renewal, if there is not going to be a revival or awakening, and if the church has lost its soul, then, again, why write at all? First, to give a wake-up call to the few who will be blessed to discover the fullness of joy and peace that accompany a life of sacrifice and service, a way of life that follows the assurances of grace and forgiveness in Christ. Second, because of our flawed and negative witness as disciples, precious souls who do not know our Savior, are being lost. Finally, a word of encouragement needs to be shared with frustrated and discouraged preachers who have not understood a critical issue is the discussion of why the church and their congregations aren't winning more souls for Christ.

Continuing to write is a statement of trust and faithfulness. It is not intended to be an expression of hope. I am fully aware that this book isn't going to serve as a catalyst for even moderate change. Since I really don't have hope that much of anything will change, perhaps I should be one of those old pastors who go out into God's pasture and try to find peace and contentment by reaching out to the suffering, the forgotten, and the destitute, who would be blessed and appreciative of someone who remembers them and just touches their lives by faithfully remembering them with a visit. I could do that.

Will renewal, passion, faithfulness, dedication, and commitment continue to happen in small ways in the church? Certainly! A few Christians will live exemplary lives as faithful disciples. Maybe some congregations or a denomination will teach their members what a disciple looks like and how to start living like one. Could there possibly be a small measure of awakening and revival? I've given up on that happening. As soon as I finish writing, I will get on with serving "the least of these," going on more walks with my wife, taking her to theatre more often, spending more time with our kids and grandkids, traveling while we still have the time and energy, reading in our screened-in gazebo or my recliner, getting under the skin of my wife's sisters Sandy and Bev- especially Sandy. That's my bucket list. This is all good stuff, no, great stuff, and I can't wait to do more of it. But if that's all there is, it would be easy for me to get too attached to a couple of Manhattan's starting in the late afternoon in order to numb the pain of the emptiness and meaninglessness.

There has to be more, and there is. I will write, and what happens, happens. Then, together with my wife Karen we will find those areas of ministry where our lives can touch the hurts and hearts of those around us. We'll sit in our recliners and try to remember each other's names. I will keep on saying sweet things, and she will respond with the smile and twinkle in her eye that have always melted my heart. And I will continue to tilt at spiritual windmills with every ounce of energy I can muster, and with a heart for the Lord that is always renewed and refreshed by Him. The days will be blessed. Love will be shared. And our fellowship in the Lord will be celebrated now and for all eternity.

My brother says any effort always has to lead to action, that what we do has to lead to getting something done. We need to build coalitions of those who see it the way we do, and are willing to work together to change things. At this point, what I can do right now is make people stop and think, and reflect, and perhaps consider revaluating the constructs of their current understanding of the church.

There was a time when I really did not want to write this at all. I don't want to argue or convince anyone of its validity any more than is done here. I really don't want to defend it. I don't want to deal with the intensity and anger of those whose reality and beliefs are threatened by it. I am at peace with where I am now, acknowledging my sinfulness and owning my brokenness, but coming to terms with it as one who is blessed by forgiveness in Christ. All I pray for is that there can be a passionate, yet reasoned and respectful conversation. As always, when we are in conversation with those who are upset with us and lose control, it is our responsibility to listen and try to understand. I pray for the patience to be able to listen courteously and respectfully to those who see all of this differently than I do. With the help of the Holy Spirit, I will seek to understand them and learn from them. I will try to remember that deep down they, too, are on a spiritual journey, where their rants and outbursts are the cries of despair of those desperately searching for more.

When I share this with others, especially the clergy, there will be resistance. There are those who will certainly take exception to what I have to say. But that is a good thing. If I am off base, if I am all wet, or if I am not being faithful to the teachings of the Bible, then I need to be called out. So, now what? I have to be faithful to my conscience in terms of how I understand what the Scriptures teach. If this is the way I see it, and this is what I believe to be true, and if it addresses an issue that I believe is critical for the life of the church, then it has to be said.

There is certainly no desire or intent to disrespect or marginalize the magnificent efforts of those who love and serve the Lord with zeal and commitment. They are an inspiration to me and encourage me in the faith in ways that can't be measured. There have been myriads of them throughout the history of the church. They labor in anonymity and obscurity in the back yards of our cities and in mission fields throughout the world. Their faithfulness is a joy to behold. One could go on and on listening to their stories without ever tiring of them.

What's happening is that the cumulative impact of their ministry, together with that of faithful church members and clergy everywhere, is hardly making a dent in the accomplishment of our mission. The world around us hardly notices the church anymore, and those who do notice don't have a favorable opinion of us.

Sure, the church makes a difference in the lives of our members; the church means a great deal to us. Yet, the message of the Gospel is not inspiring us and transforming us into dynamic disciples. We are not sharing the blessing of the wonderful message we have come to believe with others. We lack the passion and dedication to commit ourselves to lives of sacrifice and service. Certainly, we are able to reach a few – relatively, a very few. Not that each person we reach isn't important, but that isn't the issue. We have not come anywhere near living up to our potential and have failed to take advantage of our window of opportunity. Facing the truth about myself and the church was truly a "come to Jesus" moment.

Much of the Old Testament is the record of the unfaithfulness of God's chosen people, the children of Israel. Through His prophets God repeatedly pleads with his people to be faithful to the covenant they entered into with Him on Mt. Sinai. God communicated the terms of the agreement through Moses: "Now therefore, if you will indeed obey my voice and keep my covenant, you shall be my treasured people among all peoples. . ." (Exodus 19:5). They responded by promising, "All that the Lord has spoken, we will do" (Exodus 19:8). God's profound grief and sadness was rooted in their unfaithfulness to Him after all He had done for them. He secured their release after four-hundred years of slavery in Egypt, opened the Red Sea so they could cross and escape the Egyptian army, made daily provision for them by supplying an ample amount of unleavened bread and quail, and still, His wayward people did not abide by the terms of their end of the covenant. Their unfaithfulness in carrying out their part of the covenant broke His heart.

Now it has happened again. Those outside the community of faith find precious little to respect about us. God is also getting tired of our excuses and mediocrity, fed up with our unfaithfulness to follow through on our part of the New Testament covenant, where we are to be a light to the world. We have broken His heart yet again.

Israel didn't need to be reminded of her election as God's people. She believed it all too well, confident that God would bless her no matter what she did. In a nutshell, her understanding of covenant and election became mechanical. She forgot that the covenant was a bilateral agreement, requiring the worship of God alone and strict obedience to His righteous law. Her's was a history of God's grace, repaid by gross ingratitude. In much the same way, the New Testament covenant relationship of the church to our Lord has become mechanical. We, too, have received God's grace. We believe that God will bless us no matter what we do or don't do. We don't think our sins are all that bad anyway. From our point of view, not following up by being faithful disciples isn't all that big a deal.

In this chapter, I have described what happened, in my experience, once I realized that the church has failed miserably to be faithful in responding to all that the Lord has done for us. It has been a rude awakening. Nevertheless, what I do know, for certain, is that God is gracious and merciful, abounding in love, and always ready to forgive.

Being struck with a picture of the church that is quite different than I thought it was, quite different than what God called it to be, was quite a shock. Realizing that the church is only a shadow of what it was intended to be is very disturbing. It's like the church has lost the very essence of what it is that gives it life. The church has lost its soul.

I felt very much alone. This is not the description of a church that most people see. In one way, I was eager to start conversations about all of this right away. In another way, I was not. Actually, there was no choice. It was time to try to gather my thoughts, write them down as soon as possible, and then have conversations with those who might be interested. As of now, that is the plan. At age 77, I only have so much time left to serve Him. I hope that this narrative will offer some direction for a conversation that is long overdue in the church and allow me to get back to serving "the least of these" in His name.

Chapter 2

The "Invisible" Church

I can't find you! Where are you hiding? Come on. Where are you?

I can't find it! I can't find the Church! Come on. Where are you hiding?

"Ollie, Ollie Oxenfree!"

We would expect that it is the church that would be out front dominating the news every day. "Look at what the church is doing here. Wow!" "Look at what the church is doing over there." "Can you believe what the church is doing?"

The world around us hardly notices the church. They see church buildings all over, but they don't see us. Most of the time we do our thing on the sidelines in obscurity and anonymity. Recently a friend told me about the ghost ants in Florida and how funny they look when moving around with their clear bodies and black feet. She said it was quite a sight. The movement of those tiny black feet taking little steps is the only way we know they're there. It seemed like an apt metaphor for expressing my concerns about the church. We see some little feet moving about and doing ministry here and there. But for the most part, the church is invisible.

The church is missing in action. In the course of our daily lives, if family, friends, neighbors, and co-workers didn't know we were Christians and members of the church, they probably couldn't tell. Most of the time, people can't tell Christians from non-Christians or the churched from the unchurched. We look and act pretty much like everybody else. While we should be easily identified, we're not. We should be the ones that stand out. It just isn't happening. The church has lost its soul.

"Ollie, ollie oxenfree!" We remember yelling those words as kids when we played "hide-and-seek." It is what we yelled when we couldn't find someone. It indicated to our friends who were hiding that they could safely come out into the open. After trying to find the church for a long time, I feel like yelling, "Ollie, Ollie Oxen Free!" Come out into the open where I can see you.

Soul

The soul is thought of as the essence of a person, that which makes a person a living being. People do not possess the source of life and the possibility of continued existence in themselves. Adam became a living soul when God "breathed into his nostrils the breath of life" (Genesis 2:7). The soul is an entity conceived of as being the essence of life or of the individual. It is thought of as the essence that makes something what it is. I will use the term to convey the essence of the church, the body of Christ.

And what is that essence? Given what we Christians claim we believe about Jesus, we would expect to stand out in stark contrast to the world around us. We would expect church people to be noticeably different from the general population. The truth is that we aren't. We don't live up to the high ideals we say we stand for. We don't practice what we preach. We don't live our lives simply and frugally, so that we have more resources available to meet the needs of others. We don't follow Christ's commands very well at all. Christians living out the biblical model of discipleship are few and far between. We are not all that different from everybody else. The Christian world is actually pretty small, to the point that we're almost invisible. Most people do not even notice that we are out there. If we lived lives characterized by compassion, sacrifice, and service, the world would notice and ask why. It would quickly and easily figure out that we are different because we have something really special.

The church has been almost totally absorbed by the culture. Everyone goes about their business with precious little, if any, awareness of the church. In their daily lives, people are oblivious to the church. Life goes on. We see church advertised in the newspaper but don't see it in the lives of our neighbors and co-workers. The visible church is almost invisible.

When we stop and think about it, and pray about it, we can clearly see the reality of how the church is viewed by the world. The church is valued by the government and the powers that be because it helps to establish the moral compass of our nation. The foundation of our Judeo-Christian tradition is understood to be the "Ten Commandments." That's all it is valued for! That's it! Many "poke fun" at, or are critical of and hostile toward the church for beliefs they consider to be archaic, outdated, and unscientific. In terms of the value and meaning of the church's commitment to its primary mission, the church is viewed with increasing antagonism. The world puts up with us. The world throws us a bone every now and then. How did we get here? How did this happen? Is there an explanation? This is how this very sorry state of affairs came to be.

We quickly and clearly see that, given what we Christians claim to believe about Jesus, we would expect that it would make a dramatic difference in our lives; church people would look noticeably different from the general population. There wouldn't be much difficulty in spotting us, but this just isn't happening. We blend in very nicely with the rest of the people in our society – thank you. We wouldn't want to be labeled religious fanatics or anything like that, now would we?

Bringing everything into focus is difficult, given that it's almost like we're invisible. I'm not talking about church buildings, the spires on cathedrals in our cities, or steeples on churches that dot the landscape in small towns and villages across our country. They are everywhere. If that's what we mean by visible, then yeah, we can be seen all over. Despite what would be the protestations of the large majority of church members, for all practical purposes, the church is invisible, even with the tall steeples of stately old churches. Yet, when it comes to living lives of humble, sacrificial service, that stand in stark contrast to the rest of the population, we have to look a whole lot harder. At present, we have thousands and thousands of churches, but very little visibility and influence. If all of us were to come alive, the rest of the population would notice and figure out why we're excited and involved in sacrificial service.

We would expect the church to be visible, and it is almost invisible. We go to our churches to worship, for weddings and for funerals, but we do not stand out and make a great impression because of our service to the poor, needy, destitute, and homeless.

We would expect the church to be full of joy and smiles and laughter.
Too often, the tone is one of reverence and frowns.

We would expect the church to be vibrant.
Where there should be a buzz, the place is somber.

We expect Christians to be excited.
Instead, we're complaining about the moral decay in our nation.

What in the world is going on?
Am I speaking in hyperbole and overstating the case? Yes, but not by much.

We would expect to meet church people everywhere we go.
Instead, we have to try to find where they are hiding.

We would expect the church to be so much more than it is.
In truth, it is less than we would have ever thought.

We would expect the church to be serving all in need.
In truth, it serves only a few.

What in the world is going on?

Am I speaking in hyperbole and overstating the case? Yes, but not by much.

We expect the church to be on fire.

We realize it is just "blowing smoke."

The church acts like it is more important than it is.

Humility is often a forgotten virtue.

We would expect the church to be visible, and it is almost invisible.

We would expect the church to be everywhere, and it is nowhere.

What in the world is going on?

Am I speaking in hyperbole and overstating the case? Yes, but not by much.

I would have expected the church to be so much more. It just doesn't compute.

The culture is a moral mess. I get that. What I don't get is how dismally we have failed in trying to influence our culture. Tragically, we've gone about it in the wrong way. If we are speaking in terms of our impact on the culture, the visible church is almost invisible. What's this all about? For a long time I didn't get it. Now I think I do. We see a little of the church here and there, but where is the rest of it? Help me find it. Please! Help me find it! How all of this impacts the culture is what this book hopes to unpack. The few bright lights need the rest of us to let "This Little Gospel Light of Mine" shine, if we are to make a difference. It's just not happening.

We have been almost completely absorbed into what's going on in the world around us. Whether it's at the shopping mall, the Dollar Store, Best Buy, Costco, the Little League field, or where we work, we're just not a part of what's going on. While editing this chapter one morning at Burger King, the conversation between two retirees in the next booth went from bowling, to the casino, to playing cards, to golf, and finally to winters in Florida. For many retirees, this is their world. This is what they worked hard for and saved for all those years. Young folks today may make brief stops at our churches for weddings and funerals, but many don't even know what we are referring to when they see the signs in our yards that say "Keep Christ in Christmas." Many more don't know what Easter is about. They don't know the very basics of the Christian faith. Today, many have parents who never went to church or who stopped going when they were young, so the kids are never brought to worship or even Sunday school.

I have attended a great conference sponsored by a local Lutheran foundation for several years. Attendees want to get some ideas about what they could do to take up the challenge to "Change or Die." The leaders are gifted, dedicated, and passionate. Recently, it dawned on me that the paradigm of the larger church, on which they are building models for ministry, is flawed. Small outposts of the church here and there will show signs of vitality in fits and spurts, but we are a far cry from awakening and renewal. In reality, we are pretty much invisible.

Our primary identity is with the rank and file of laity and clergy, rather than the few exceptions who are shining examples, whose lives of discipleship are characterized by sacrifice and service. Except for the steeples that rise up over Milwaukee and in the countryside all across America, the church doesn't have much of a presence. We are unrelated and irrelevant to almost everything that is happening around us. We are a dinosaur. We are a relic of the past. We mean nothing to most everybody. We mean something to almost nobody. We are invisible. We have lost our soul.

The church describes itself in high sounding, glowing terms, while underneath there is little real substance. The solid rock on which we stand is Christ. However, His church has become an empty shell. Some may say that I'm being disrespectful to my Lord and my God. Some may emphatically reject what I'm saying. I really want to be wrong – totally.

I really want things to be different from the way I see them. Then I tell myself, "Dream on." As I see the church, it is being disrespectful and playing fast and loose with the Gospel. It is the church that disrespects the world to which it ministers. The church has lost its bearings. The church has lost its way. The church has deviated significantly from the mission to which it was called. And I'm not referring to the family spats about doctrine, where we all defend our teaching as truth. No, we have all strayed far from the course. Nevertheless, we are so committed to the way we are going and what we are doing that making enough of a course correction that would give a flicker of hope that the church might once again become the holder of the torch of joy, meaning, purpose, and peace for the world is not even an option.

The church is a lightweight, a little leaguer, small time, a joke. Oops. I'd better not say that: God might be listening. On second thought, He already knows. Once before His people let Him down big time after they had promised, "All that the Lord has spoken, we will do." He knows, and He is devastated. It breaks His heart.

"And They Call Themselves Christians"

This is a comment we hear all the time. It is the clearest way of expressing that non-Christians, and even our own kids, have been turned off by the church. It doesn't help to explain to those who point to the hypocrites as their reason for not wanting to go to church, that hypocrites are weak Christians, still struggling with what it means to be a disciple. We do not wink at un-Christian behavior. If we know about it and do wink at it, that's on us, and we need to be held accountable.

So what's the bottom line? Which of the following says it best?
- The church has lost its soul, and it doesn't look like it will be getting it back any time soon.
- Where are our "better angels?"
- The church has sold its soul.
- The church has lost its soul and likely won't get it back.
- The church has lost its soul, and any hope of getting it back is only a pipedream.

Without question, it is the last option. Very few outside the church listen to us. Very few outside the church pay much attention to us.

We Christians have always considered the church to be a great, noble, and holy institution. We all want to believe the best about the church. It is extremely disturbing and painful the first time we are overcome by an awareness of the magnitude of the church's monumental failure to live up to its calling, to live up to what we always thought it was, to live up to its holy purpose and high ideals. We are shocked, stunned, and saddened. Our whole world is shattered. Almost all of what is at the heart and core of everything we believed about the church vanishes, as if it was all an illusion. Our reason for being and some of our core beliefs are called into question, and need to be thoroughly reviewed and reconsidered.

As we watch and observe what people are doing and where they are going, more than likely the church isn't a part of it. And we wonder why? It is my hope that this book will be a part of the conversation that seeks to understand "why." The church is so out of touch. The church is so out of the mainstream. We're living life in a bubble. We've created our own history and reality. We tell it to each other, we believe it, and we live in this product of our own imagination. Coming to this awareness is one of those moments when we feel like the earth is moving beneath us and we are shaken to the core. At that point I was blessed with another level of awareness and clarity. I realized that I had unintentionally been misled. We have many sincere and dedicated church leaders who are indeed trying to move the church in a direction that is faithful to its New Testament roots, who have taken a drink of the "Kool-Aid" that distorts reality.

We all search for meaning, purpose, and truth in our lives, and sometimes we find them. Sometimes we reject the truth we have found, choosing instead to live life our way, within the belief system we have already created for ourselves, while trying to find some way to rationalize or reframe our choice in a futile attempt to have it both ways. Tragically, we are fooling nobody but ourselves, and in the process, miss the opportunity to find real meaning and purpose. This has happened to enough of us that the church has lost its soul and become invisible.

Our child wanders away in a store, and we can't find him. It's more than panic. It's sheer terror. We scream, "Where's my child? Has anyone seen my child?" Our fear and distress is unbearable! "Please God, help me find my child." Where's my church? Has anyone seen my church? I've lost my church! I can't find my church! It's invisible. Coming to the awareness that our church has become invisible and gotten lost is sheer terror.

Here is the way in which we, and the world around us, can identify the church. John 15:12 says, "This is my commandment, that you love one another as I have loved you." Matthew 5:16 reads, "Let your light shine before others, so that they may see your good works and give glory to your Father who is in heaven." There, we found it. We know where it is. It doesn't have to be invisible anymore. Now it's up to us to share the Gospel and live a life of sacrifice and service so we can help others make the invisible church a place which gives the ultimate in peace, comfort, and joy in living and serving. There, we've found it, and we can't return to life as it was. As God's people, we are called to serve. We are called to connect with the needs of the world around us as we live out our Christian lives.

The church isn't seen much today. All of what the church says in blaming the culture for the moral decay of the nation and the decline of the church is nothing more than a deflection from the real reasons why we have become invisible. We had a chance to do something about human need, pain, suffering, and misery, and we dropped the ball. We just don't find many believers who have given heed to the Scriptures' call to completely surrender their life to Christ.

We Christians have the task of representing and reflecting our loving God. This is the church's mission. What kind of representatives are we if Monday through Saturday and much of Sunday, we are invisible; that is, our lives don't look all that different from others in our culture. If we are just as self-serving and self-centered as everybody else, why would anyone pay attention to us, let alone want to join the family of faith?

We are not challenged to the life of commitment, dedication, and faithful service characteristic of mature faith. When we are not living that way, the world notices. They watch us and they wonder why. Those who are not members of the church do not see the differences they would expect to see in our lives based on what we claim to believe about a loving, accepting, and self-sacrificing God who died on the cross in our place and as our substitute in order that we might be assured of forgiveness and eternal life. Part of the reason non-Christians resent our efforts to evangelize is because of our hypocrisy in the difference between what we say we believe and what they see in our lives. They just don't see many faithful Christians in action, loving, caring, and serving. They understandably conclude that we are spiritually and morally bankrupt. It's no wonder that we're invisible. So, how does one go about describing the new reality of the church as clearly and forthrightly as possible, speaking hard truth and making assertions that no doubt will be considered outrageous and unjustified by an overwhelming majority of Christians?

Chapter 3

Good Works – We Can't Ever Do Enough

We can't ever do enough good works. Most would understand this to mean that we can't do enough good works to please God, that we can't do enough good works to earn God's favor, and that we can't do enough good works to earn our way to heaven. I'm using it to convey that once we come to believe in Christ and all He has done for us so we can be forgiven and assured of eternal life, we are overwhelmed by God's mercy, blown away, and transformed. We change dramatically. We can't ever do enough to show how much we love Him.

Why Do We Do "Good Works?"

Doing good works are central to the Christian life in all denominations and expressions of Christianity. We all emphasize the importance of holy living. Mother Teresa is usually lifted up as the ultimate example.

Within the historical context of the New Testament, the author of Hebrews reminds us of the supremacy of Christ and the all-sufficiency of His work. He reminds us of the treasure we have in Christ, then applies these truths to the lives of his readers,. He says, in effect, "Now that you've got this treasure, what are you going to do with it?" He reminds us of the blessings that are ours in Christ and makes it clear that the appropriate response is a life of faithful service. Look what Christ did for us. Now, we can't do enough to serve Him. This service is not coerced or demanded. It is offered joyfully, freely, and willingly.

The foundation of our good works is the forgiveness that is ours through Christ's suffering and death on the cross. Our good works are done in response to being given the free and undeserved gifts of forgiveness, life, and salvation. We serve the Lord, not because we have to, but because we want to. We don't do good works in order to get to heaven, but because we have already been given the gift of heaven.

As noted, Christianity is defined by, and identified by, two core beliefs, the Trinity and the person of Christ, that He is both true God and true man. Beyond these core beliefs, there are many variations and nuances in what we believe and teach, which account for the many different denominations that have developed since the Reformation. Some believe there is a spark of goodness in man that reaches out to God, while others believe that we are unable to initiate a relationship with Him because of our depraved, sinful condition. Some teach that the sacraments symbolize or represent important spiritual truth, while others teach that they are efficacious means of grace through which God works faith. Some hold that "once saved, always saved," while others believe we can fall away from the faith. Some say that healing miracles still happen today, while others say they stopped happening after the early days of the church. Some believe that Christ died for all people who have ever lived. Others believe He died only for those who will be saved.

However, one teaching that crosses all denominational lines is the importance of doing good works. Good works are done because of what has been done for us, as the joyful response to having already been given the gift of heaven. The good works we do are the means through which God is at work in the world through His church. "For Christ's love compels us, because we are all convinced that one died for all, and therefore all died. And He died for all, that those who live should no longer live for themselves but for Him who died for them and was raised again" (2 Corinthians 5:14, 15, NIV). What is it above all else that compels Paul to carry out his ministry with such passion and devotion? What comes first is Christ's love for him. Christ's love for us always precedes our response, which is to show our love for Him by loving others in His name.

All denominations and expressions of Christianity teach the importance of doing good works and encourage their practice. Scripture teaches that we are to go out as Christ into the world and "as we have opportunity, do good to all people, especially to those who belong to the family of believers" (Galatians 6:10, NIV), to "love one another" (John 15:12) as He has loved us, and to "love your neighbor as yourself" (Matthew 22:39).

The Lord's righteous deeds to save sinners inspire us to do good deeds in service to others. Faith first receives the free gifts of forgiveness and salvation that God gives by grace, and then responds as led by the Holy Spirit. We show our love for Christ through lives of service to others. Our good deeds always follow. Our faith always bears fruit by leading us to serve our neighbor.

Luther knew that faith looks very different on paper than it does in the flesh, where it is: "a living, busy, active, mighty thing, this faith. It is impossible for us not to be doing good works incessantly. It does not ask whether good works are to be done, but before the question is asked, it has already done them, and is constantly doing them."[4]

Yet, tragically and with devastating consequences, the church has failed to teach and emphasize the importance of living the transformed life of gratitude and service in response to all He has done for us. When a person has faith, we can see it in their works. Where there is faith, it bears fruit. Since God has loved and served us with a self-giving, self-sacrificing, selfless life and death, we eagerly and joyfully seek to make a major course correction by living lives of self-giving, self-sacrificing, selfless love and service to others.

When the Holy Spirit opens up the Scriptures to us and we become aware of what it means to be a disciple, we begin making the radical adjustments necessary to carry out the full commitment we have made. There is no going half-way. We commit to study and learn what a full commitment means, and then pray for the spiritual strength to be able to implement these changes. The church has flat-out failed to place enough emphasis upon the importance of living a spiritually renewed life, working for charity and justice for people in need.

The Bible sets the bar as high as it will go when establishing a guide for living. With the help of the Holy Spirit, we try as hard as we can to imitate the self-giving, self-sacrificing, selfless love of Christ as a response to all He has done for us. He gave his life as a sacrifice on a cross for our sins so that we might have the extraordinary gifts of forgiveness and eternal life. With the Spirit's help, we keep seeking new understanding of the magnitude of His gifts and blessings and more insight into the specifics of our response.

We are overjoyed and ready to respond and get involved in loving service, sharing the Gospel and doing what we can to serve the lost, the last, the least, and the lonely. We seek to live out our lives showing kindness and compassion, meeting the needs of our neighbor. Yet, it doesn't compute that way in our heads, hearts, and souls. What Christ did for us doesn't make hardly any difference at all. The current state of affairs should be such that the scarcity of good works would totally blow our minds, but it doesn't. This is what we have come to expect as the norm for the Christian life. Day in and day out we seek healing, encouragement, and comfort. Day after day we continue living life as if it is business as usual.

Then one day God's word stirs powerfully within us and it all hits us. Our justifications and rationalizations come tumbling down, and we see ourselves in all of our meanness and selfishness.

When, after facing our meanness and selfishness, we are suddenly "presented with the Gospel which promises us that we will not be shamed or scolded or punished or shunned but instead flooded with His love [. . .], the Holy Spirit [. . .] takes our heart in his hands, and gives us the courage to face ourselves as we really are. Why does He do it? So 'you will know the truth and the truth will set you free [John 8:32].'"5 Pure joy washes over us! Thankfulness fills us! In our new freedom, we look to the same Spirit for the strength to give our all to Him in lives of good works, in lives of sacrifice, and in lives service. "Let us not love in word or talk but in deed and in truth" (I John 3:18).

Do we do works to witness, because God commanded that we do them, or because people are hurting? The bottom line is that God commanded that we do good works because people are hurting, and He wants to help them through us. The bottom line is that God wants us to sacrificially serve those who are in need. However, as already noted, God also uses our good works and sacrificial service to lead others to come to know Him and to give glory to Himself.

Good Works Scarce Among Christians

Then comes the kicker, the sad but astonishing truth that while all denominations teach good works, we all rationalize and compromise the full truth of God's command to do them and come up short when it comes to living out this command. The similarity of outcomes in response to the teaching of good works is freaky. Good works are scarce among Christians. We just wouldn't expect it to be the case. Examples of sacrificial service are hard to find. It seems as if there is collusion to perpetuate the ordinary. Faith without works is a counterfeit expression of the Gospel, trying to substitute something of less value for the real deal. Our efforts aren't much. They don't come anywhere near that of which we are capable.

If we just want to be decent, respectable folks, that's one thing. Being kind, caring, and compassionate in a way that reflects a concern that goes to the very depth of our being, involves sacrifice, and defines who we are, is a whole different ballgame. Those who have a deep and abiding concern for the needs of all of humanity, and a willingness to make a sacrificial commitment to do everything possible to alleviate human need and suffering, are few. Our sinful nature keeps us from making a whole-hearted commitment. It keeps us from devoting ourselves to a life of showing our love for God through a life of selfless service to others. We just don't want to make that much of a sacrifice. We don't have to be rich, but we would like to enjoy a few of the perks which God provides in abundance.

It doesn't seem to matter what a denomination teaches about good works. We all come up short. Living lives of dedicated service is the exception rather than the rule. Our good works don't amount to much.

They are little more than window dressing. What we all do is a pittance compared to what we could do. Even those of us who are convinced we get it right in our doctrine, get it wrong when it comes to our response to all that God has done for us and when it comes to living out those teachings. Our underperformance stands in stark contrast to the biblical description of lives of dedicated, loving service. Together we are spiritually bankrupt - a veritable wasteland of good works.

People in need could be served, but aren't. The suffering could be helped and comforted, but it doesn't happen. The forgotten could be visited and the abandoned could be found, but we're "too busy." Because of our inaction, there are millions out there who are falling by the wayside.

We are drastically underemphasizing the importance and centrality of good works and of living the life of faithful servants as dedicated disciples. "For by grace you have been saved through faith. And this is not your own doing; it is the gift of God, not a result of works, so that no one may boast. For we are his workmanship, created in Christ Jesus for good works, which God prepared beforehand, that we should walk in them" (Ephesians 2:8-10). We have detached the last verse from the previous two. We stand convicted in a court-martial for dereliction of duty. Yet, we don't see it; obviously, we are not being convicted by our sin and do not fully grasp the implications of Christ's dying on the cross as our substitute.

A Standard for Measuring Good Works

We all have some thoughts about whether we're doing enough good works or at least coming close to doing enough. But how do we make that evaluation? Is the standard by which we measure ourselves that of our culture, our religious tradition, or some combination of both? Do we choose the standard we use for evaluating good works, or do we adopt the generally agreed upon cultural norm for good works? We need to understand that using the cultural norm leads to an inflated estimation of our efforts. While we may be hard-working, decent people, that's light years away from practicing a life of simplicity, frugality, sacrifice, and service. We often do just enough good works to satisfy our consciences and convince ourselves that we meet, and even exceed, cultural norms for doing good works.

When we say that we can see love, compassion, mercy, commitment, dedication, caring, and service in the hearts and lives of many donors and volunteers, it sounds awesome. However, if we want to be honest with ourselves, we have to make an effort to be precise. I'll use a scale of 1-100. One designates a person whose level of good works, charitable contributions, and volunteer work is the least possible, and 100 is Christ, who gave His all for us on the cross. Ninety-nine is the person who can't do enough good works, gives away all they absolutely don't need, and is always ready to serve.

There are many decent people who are helpful neighbors and good citizens, contribute something to church and charity, and, occasionally, volunteer. It would seem to me that this group would fall at level 16. My assessment is an eye opener for most, who consider it excessively harsh or even punitive. Level 31 would be those who have moved to the place where they give 5-10 percent of their income to church and charity and volunteer an average of 4-6 hours per month. Level 43 might be those who contribute 10 percent of their income to church and charity, and volunteer 6-8 hours per month. Then, let's say there is a single mom working two jobs, raising a 16-year-old son and an 11-year-old daughter, offering many hours of her time as a volunteer, and is also generous in her charitable giving. She exceeds what it usually looks like when people with full, busy lives make a significant, sacrificial commitment to a life of service. Rather than being selfish and content with a life of selective inattention to suffering, hunger, poverty, and need, she is higher on the scale because of her sacrifice. Let's say she is at level 68. We'll put Mother Teresa at level 96 rather than 99, only because she herself had acknowledged her sins, shortcomings, and unworthiness.

Many Bible passages make it clear what it means to bear fruit, to do good works. After we look at them in Chapter 6, we can evaluate ourselves again. For now, suffice it to say, we tend to evaluate ourselves much too favorably. We do not demonstrate the "grateful devotion" of dedicated disciples.

It goes without saying that any good work is significant and important. There are no small deeds of kindness, compassion, service, or charity. Every small good work is indeed a blessing to the one who has been helped and served. When evaluating ourselves, however, my concern is that we only do a little when we are capable of doing so much more.

Faith Active in Love is All That Matters

These words are from a wall-plaque that I've had in my study, and cherished as a reminder, since my first parish. I have to admit that the fullness of its meaning is still in the process of becoming clear. Galatians 5:6 (NIV) says, "The only thing that counts is faith expressing itself through love." We are indeed God's own people, and, as such, we are all too eager to see ourselves as "special." Are we just like the Old Testament people of God who felt they had some special status because they were children of Abraham? We have been delivered through the sacrifice of God's own Son, the Messiah, and given a new beginning, in a new community of faith, the church. That's already happened. But I am suggesting that Jesus sees us the way he saw the Pharisees and Sadducees who reveled in their being God's chosen people, the Children of Abraham.

What has to be made clear is that it is our sins that nailed Christ to the cross, and that in joyful, willing response, we offer all that we are and all that we have to Him in return. We are no longer our own. When the Lord claims us, we live for Him and serve Him with all of our being. Colossians 3 teaches that we belong to God. Yet, some come to church and leave with the attitude, "I'll see you next Sunday." The call to show our love for God by loving our neighbor all week long is the farthest thing from their mind. For them, living as a Christian means that we are going to try to avoid any major moral slip-ups. Rather, in faith, we no longer belong to ourselves. We dedicate our lives to showing love for God by loving and serving our neighbor.

In order to be able to influence the world around us, in order for others to notice our good works and be curious, interested or attracted enough to want to know why we live the way we do, and in order to be credible, there have to be transformational changes in the way we Christians live. Up until now, we haven't even come close to getting the world's attention and influencing its thinking. We have been a monumental and tragic failure. In our preaching and teaching, we speak mostly about minor stuff, not the really big issues or the overarching sins. We don't hear much about how we have not come close to living as totally dedicated, totally committed disciples, and that we aren't the good Christians we think we are. We don't stand out as people who live exemplary lives of sacrifice and service.

We totally understate the importance of good works. "Why do you call me, 'Lord, Lord,' and do not do what I say? I will show you what he is like who comes to me and hears my words and puts them into practice. He is like a man building a house, who dug down deep and laid the foundation on rock. . ." (Luke 6:46-48, NIV). This is good stuff!

The biblical position is that good works are the fruits of faith. We often hear that the focus should be on the root of the Gospel and the fruits will naturally follow. I don't think so! Without defining the self-denial and sacrifice implicit in discipleship and an explanation of what the fruits of faith look like, they don't naturally follow. This misleading assertion is a significant contributing factor in the church losing its soul.

When people come to faith, do the fruits naturally follow? Naturally? It depends on what we mean by "naturally." If we are referring to a token response, then yes. If we are talking about the response of a totally committed disciple, that's a whole different issue. We'll thoroughly address what a totally dedicated disciple looks like in chapters 5, 6 and 7. For now, suffice it to say that we have been far too casual in the way we have been teaching what it looks like when a disciple is doing good works. We are forgiven, but we immediately resume making compromises with sin and continue to live lives with a self-centered, self-seeking, and self-serving orientation. Given this tendency, faith doesn't naturally bear fruit. What usually follows are half-hearted attempts. Good works follow strengthening the root through the Word only if strengthening the root includes clearly teaching what it means to live the life of a totally committed disciple.

Recently, I heard a pastor refer to his grandmother as an example of someone who everyone who knows her would agree is an outstanding Christian; she is different - always praying and reading the Bible. From my perspective, she needs to be included in the sphere of my concern. In her case, the issue is the difference in the definition of what it means to be pious and what it means to be a disciple. She may well have dedicated her life to doing so much more, but for her, the bar has just been set way too low. The tree isn't bearing much fruit. I shared my heart with him with all of the empathy and understanding I could muster. His response was that he is convinced that we just have to keep the sequence in the proper order: keep strengthening the root through the Word, and the good works will follow. Yes, while I agree that we have to keep the sequence in the proper order, namely, what precedes and what follows, what if grandma has learned only a minimalist, compromised, and watered-down version of what it means to be a Christian, to do good works, and to be a disciple?

We all want Jesus as our Savior, but we don't want to be asked to do too much, let alone commit our lives to Him. We want to hear all about Jesus being Savior of our souls, but not too much about Him being Lord of our lives.

Chapter 4

The Church: Deteriorating, Decaying, and Dying

The world is questioning and searching for meaning and purpose. It always has been and it always will be. God's intention is for people to look at us, be led to faith in Christ and then praise and magnify His name because of what they see in us. John 13:34, 35 says, "A new commandment I give to you, that you love one another: just as I have loved you, so you are to love one another. By this all people will know that you are my disciples, if you have love for one another." Also, Matthew 5:16 says, "Let your light shine before others, that they may see your good works and give glory to your Father who is in heaven." When others look at us, they need to see God. They need to get an idea of what God is like. We wear the brand and carry the reputation of the parent company. When God's name is lifted up in our lives, the rest of the world will come to know what a fantastic, loving God we have. That's just not happening, and the church is in the midst of a serious decline.

The Numbers Don't Lie

"In the early 1950's, [. . .] people across the country started to go to church en masse."[6] After holding steady for a while, the trend began to reverse itself. According to a 2014 Barna Report, 51 percent of U.S. adults say, "Church attendance is not important." "General church attendance has been on the decline for the past two decades in America and nearly one-third of Millennials who grew up in church have dropped out at some point."[7] As noted in Chapter 1, in 1973, 66% of Americans had confidence in organized religion. By 2017, it was down to 40%. In 1987, 10% of adults had no religious affiliation; today that number is 25%.[8]

People like me ("Nones") are on the rise. The "Nones," those who are not affiliated with any religion, or are agnostic, or just plain atheist, are now almost a quarter of the population, says a recent study out of Duke University. There are 19 million more "Nones" now than there were in 2007. And at 56 million strong, there are more Americans who are unaffiliated than there are Catholics and mainline Protestants, according to a 2015 Pew Research report. Fewer than half of young adults ages 18-30 are sure God exists. In a few years, the largest "religion" in the U.S. will be "None."[9]

It is astounding when we realize that it hasn't taken all that long for this dramatic shift to occur.

The number of people unaffiliated with any religion was mounting year after year. According to a Pew survey [. . .] the number of people who said they had no affiliation with any religion had risen from 15 percent to almost 20 percent in just five years. [. . .] 30 percent of those under thirty said they had no religious affiliation, but many older people who said they seldom or never went to church had included themselves in the category, and with few exceptions, the 'Nones' were not looking for a church to go to.[10]

In my own denomination, The Lutheran Church–Missouri Synod (LCMS), we had 2,772,648 members in 1971 and 2,270,921 in 2010, a drop of 500,000. Since the late 1950's, child baptisms are down 70 percent, and adult converts are down 47 percent.

Synod-wide membership declines. [. . .] Christians make up a smaller and smaller proportion of the American population every year (down to just 71 percent in 2017). Every District of the LCMS has experienced numerical decline in the past decade – from a 4 percent decline in some places to over 25 percent in others. [. . .] Curtis [. . .] points out that many of these challenges facing the Synod are also true for other large church bodies in the nation.[11]

There is no question that the United States "is becoming less Christian, more secular, and more unbelieving, and the rate of change is rapid. The Pew Research Center reports that from 2007 to 2014 the percentage of Americans who say they are Christian fell from 78 to 71 percent. Over the same period, the percentage of Americans who say they are atheist, agnostic, or non-religious rose from 16 to 23 percent."[12] As of March 2018, 65 percent of U.S. adults say religion is not important in their lives.[13]

Losses are now the norm for denominations of every stripe. "The United Methodist Church lost 18 percent of its worshippers from 1974 to 2012. The Southern Baptist Convention reports that it has lost over one million members in the past 10 years and that baptisms stand at a 70-year low. In a mere seven-year span, ending in 2014, the Roman Catholic Church lost three million adherents in the United States."[14]

The data is clear: American Christianity is in decline, and every major church body is experiencing it.
The Southern Baptist Convention, the great evangelical powerhouse, second in membership only to the Catholic Church began to decline after years of spectacular growth. Between 1961 and 1998 its membership had grown by 59 percent – going from fewer than ten million to nearly sixteen million, but in 1998 it experienced its first drop in membership since 1926. [. . .] In 2006 SBC reached its peak of 16.3 million members. For a denomination centered on the Great Commission the decline was a matter of profound concern for officials. [. . .] If present trends continued, the SBC membership could fall by a half by 2050 and represent 2 percent of the population, as opposed to the 6 percent it represented in the late 1980s.[15]

The Foolishness of What We Preach

There is a whole cluster of issues that "the world considers quaint, novelties of the Church's imagination or outdated figures of a pre-scientific past."[16] Our teachings are more than enough of a stumbling block in a modern, scientific world, and a significant factor in the decline.

Modern theologians and scientists believe that a collection of ancient myths form the basis for our teachings. Unbelievers look at much of what we believe as superstition. They observe that many religions include a myth about the creation of the world and man, while they believe that the world came into being as a result of a "Big Bang," rather than the intelligent design described in Genesis. They believe that the biblical account of Noah and the flood is but one of a number of ancient epics about a great flood, and they don't believe that Jonah was swallowed by a whale. They believe the church's teaching about Jesus is built around myths that emerged and developed in the minds and imaginations of the Apostles following his death, especially miracles and the resurrection. Their view is that these early myths became the core of what the church believes and teaches. We have to remember that it requires faith to accept some of our teachings as true. This is enough of a stumbling block for potential believers without it being made more difficult when our lives don't reflect that there is anything special or different about us. Then, instead of trusting the Holy Spirit to do its work through the Word to convict people of their sin and bring them to faith, we get angry and defensive.

Most defenders of Christianity also place the blame for our decline on the secular worldview pushed by leaders in the media, government, and education. We see them as undermining the biblical understanding of marriage and the family, especially, homosexuality, gay marriage, and transgenderism. "From a young age Americans are indoctrinated by their televisions and their schools to have an anti-biblical worldview on the origins of life, the meaning of the human condition, sexuality, and a hundred other topics. This puts up barriers to the Word."[17] We're angry, and we're going to do something about this. We're going to tear down these barriers.

How we deal with these barriers is key. We fail to remember that society views our religious education as indoctrination. They have a different set of presuppositions than we do. Reason is the source of their truth. Non-Christians don't share the biblical teaching that it is the Holy Spirit who brings us to faith. Being outraged, getting angry, and tearing down is the way things work in the fallen world. It is not how we do things as

Christians. It is not the path to effective witness and outreach. This is a path that turns people off, gets in the way, sabotages, and undercuts our efforts to lead non-believers to know Christ and the boundless blessings we receive in Him. This is where we have missed it. We spread the blame all over, while forgetting to first examine our own practice and witness. We have to keep on sharing the Word and living lives of sacrifice and service that non-Christians will notice and cause them to wonder what makes us tick.

The Folly of Seeking This World's Goods and Pleasures

We blame external factors, rather than looking internally. There is no mention of looking internally to see if we ourselves have contributed to the decline. If the foolishness of what we preach isn't enough to cause significant decline, the way we live is. The main reason for our being ineffective witnesses is our failure to walk the path of compassion and service. This is why Christianity in America has declined. Sure, it's complicated, but we have overlooked how the landscape of economic opportunity has changed. Without our even noticing, discipleship has been emptied of most of its meaning.

Cracks in the structure of the church started to form and then became more serious. The integrity of the walls was compromised, and the threats that secularization posed increased the pressure on these walls. The slope of the trend lines (a weakened structure and the increased pressure from the exterior) were headed in opposite directions at a dramatic pace. However, we have only looked at the pressure being exerted from the outside. We have not been paying attention to the pillars, beams, and weight bearing walls. The cracks opened even wider because of the changing economic landscape. Our rapidly expanding economy provided much more access to a middle class lifestyle and the possibility of claiming our share of the American Dream. The powerful challenges these changes posed for the church went unnoticed.

The resulting need to re-examine what it meant to be a disciple in this new landscape never happened. The opportunity for awakening and renewal passed us by at a time when the pace of change made it extremely difficult to catch up. These changes are the equivalent of a magnitude 7.5 earthquake on a "spiritual" Richter scale. This issue has not been given nearly enough weight. It has hardly been factored into the analysis of the decline of Christianity. Nevertheless, its significance cannot be underestimated. The huge impact of external pressures could have been cushioned, and its effect reduced, if we had lived lives that reflected what we say we believe.

Listening to others while at Burger King on "cyber Monday" in 2017, I couldn't help but be reminded that average folks today have a life that is in sync with a culture driven by consumer capitalism. I understand that they are "into" all of the really neat stuff –small stuff and big stuff – that is available to us in today's economy. I also understand that people have the means to purchase more stuff and enjoy more of the good life. At the same time they don't have much of a commitment to charity.

Good church folk have adapted to the consumer mentality and assimilated it into their lifestyle so well that we can't tell the Christians from the non-Christians. Rather, we don't even see that what we're doing goes down a different path than the one chosen by disciples. We are oblivious to how far we have strayed from biblical teaching about what it means to be a disciple. We kind of know that a disciple is one who has been called out to follow Christ, but it's almost to the point where we don't have a clue what the Bible means when it calls us to "follow." Truth be told, what it means to "follow" hasn't been explained to us very well at all. Then, if what it means to be a disciple is explained, we tune out the part that calls for sacrifice. We decide what parts of biblical teaching fit with our understanding of church and religion. We have constructed our own belief system, and our religion of personal preference allows us to fit in quite nicely with the brand of consumer capitalism that drives our economy and which is enjoyed by most in our culture.

The Church in Decline

When others observe our lives as Christians, they are not inspired. Increasingly, they don't want anything to do with Christianity. Tragically, I don't see any chance that the God-fearin', hymn singin', pot-luck lovin' folks in my own denomination, or any other, are going to change. One of the primary guidelines established for writing this book was to scrupulously avoid judging, blaming, or criticizing. The intent is to convey painful, heartbreaking, and devastating truth to the church in the kindest possible way. It also became clear that accomplishing this goal, while speaking in the clearest, strongest, and most forthright language, wouldn't be possible without some folks taking offense. If I say it tactfully, people won't get it and my efforts will be a waste of time.

The church has its story too. The early part is recorded in the Bible, and then it goes from the New Testament period up to the industrial revolution. The current era is a work in progress. After a long period of growth, we are now declining, and I'm not hopeful about where we go from here. Truthfully, I'm distraught about the church's prospects for the future. I'm devastated by its impotence. There isn't much happening. There is no outpouring of mercy, love, and compassion. There is not much to be excited about. There is no reason for people to take notice of us and want to become a part of our fellowship.

Many parents are pleading for an explanation as to why their kids have strayed from the faith. We have to tell them what we know. We have to explain that, without realizing it, the church has allowed the teaching of what it means to be a disciple to be compromised. We have not lived like disciples ourselves and, therefore, have not been good witnesses and examples for our kids. Our kids are not especially impressed with, and influenced by, what they see in the lives of Christians. They see the contradiction between what we claim to believe and how it is lived out in our lives. In a world defined by science and consumer capitalism, there are all kinds of powerful forces that can distract them and make them vulnerable to being pulled away from our Lord and His church. What parents are seeing is what happens when the concept of discipleship is not taught clearly and simply.

While our reasons for being totally and selflessly committed to sharing the Gospel far exceed any other motivation, our response is minimal at best. As it relates to sacrificial giving to church and charity, we are just as greedy, self-serving, and self-centered as others. We fall so far short of our calling to be reflections of a loving God that we become a stumbling block for our kids and others who are considering Christianity. There is not much difference between the way others live their lives and the way we live ours.

During confession, we say the words, but from the results in terms of change in our lives, it seems like we have said them without a sense of their gravity. We confess a few moral lapses, a little bad language, some impure thoughts, and losing our cool in relationships with those nearest and dearest to us – all good stuff to confess, but rarely is there acknowledgement of the pervasiveness of our sinfulness reflected by the lack of willing obedience as faithful disciples. In effect, what we are doing is minimizing the gravity of our sinfulness. We look at ourselves and think we're not all that bad. God looks at us and sees a wasteland of darkness.

Philip Chard, a secular writer and psychotherapist puts it this way:
An oft heard phrase at Christmas is 'Peace on Earth, goodwill to men.' [. . .] It is a wonderful and sorely needed sentiment, one that even lasts for a while when we pause from our usual mania to be with loved ones. But, in too many of us, goodwill is short-lived.

Christmas is both a secular and religious happening, but for those who embrace it as a spiritual observance, it evokes the core principles of their Christian faith. And that, sadly, is what often proves too fleeting.

That there are many compassionate Christians (and non-Christians) among us is beyond question. You can recognize them not by their displays of public piety but by their actions, those that are true to the principles of Jesus Christ [. . .] (Spiritual growth) is about intentionally embracing one's articles of faith, manifesting them in daily life and, when failing to do so, admitting that, learning from it and moving in a better direction. [. . .] So many [. . .] pay lip service to Christian precepts.[18]

There are moments when the Holy Spirit touches our hearts, and we get it. Those moments usually pass rather quickly. The good intentions to renew our commitment are there, but only a few follow through. For the rest of us, our good intentions are short-lived.

Ever since the industrial revolution in the U.S., and especially since WWII, the church has been on a path that is heading downhill. We didn't see the connection between the increasing prosperity, our witness, and the decline. The downward trend was interrupted "in the early 1950's, when people across the country started to go to church in masse."[19] However, this period of growth was temporary and only served to distort the big picture. We were lulled into complacency.

The years in which the church flourished are over. The church in America has become a clone of the church in Europe, where people visit majestic cathedrals trying to grasp the awe and grandeur of the God who inspired their construction. They are not the place where vibrant communities gather for worship every Sunday, there to be served in worship by the God who gave His own Son to suffer and die for us on the cross, and who strengthens us for lives of sacrificial service each week. The church in America has also lost its vibrancy and vitality. It is no longer a grateful community of redeemed servants who celebrate life by praising and thanking God for all He has done for us and by showing our love for God through lives of love and service. Many keep their membership on the shelf just in case there is need for a baptism, wedding, or funeral.

The splintering of the church after the Reformation is certainly understandable, given that the church is full of sinners, which, by the way, is why we are members and why we need to worship. While splintering into denominations is certainly not the preferred outcome, it's o.k. Denominational sparring is not a good thing, but it's not the worst thing either. The whole church still seeks to carry out its mission in the world. In the midst of all this, there is something awesome that we all have to share: the saving Gospel of Jesus Christ. Although we have different emphases and nuances, Jesus' death on the cross for the forgiveness of sins and the promise of eternal life are found in all of them.

Tragically, however, the same malady also inflicts us all. We all behave in a manner that is a turn-off to those we are all trying to reach with the Gospel. There are some things we all hold on to tightly, like the lifestyle of our culture and the pursuit of a share of the American Dream, which drains resources and time that could be used to serve others in Jesus' name. Consequently, our combined witness to the world gets tarnished, muted, and rendered ineffective. All of us Christians are the same. We are cut from the same cloth. We all do a woefully inadequate job of presenting a loving, humble, dynamic, and vibrant witness to a God who asks us to represent Him. We are His instruments, chosen to love, serve, and help.

The world around us has not misinterpreted what they see in our lives. People might stumble over the Gospel, but we as the church do not want that stumbling to occur because of us or because of what we have done or failed to do. We have to live our lives in a way that is a credit, not a discredit, to Christ. In the U.S. today, the church is tolerated, not respected. We are often given the opportunity to offer a token invocation at national and community events, but we are not respected. There is no reason we should be respected. There is nothing special about us. There is nothing that stands out. We look pretty much like everybody else.

If we were different, if it was clear that we were really committed to helping others, the culture would be much more likely to give us a pass and have a greater level of tolerance for some of our views about ethics and morals. They wouldn't be as critical of us or hold the disdain and contempt for us that they do. We certainly haven't done ourselves any favors. The culture understandably perceives us as being self-righteously judgmental of others, pointing out their character flaws, while overlooking the shortcomings in our own character and behavior.

Dare I say that the church is dying and no longer a viable and productive entity? Dare I suggest that the church has outlived its usefulness? Can it survive in any meaningful way? I doubt it. It will continue to decline. We have lost our identity. We have lost our soul. We spend lots of time studying the Bible and blaming all of our problems on the moral decay in our culture, while the level of our volunteer service to the poor, needy, and lonely is minimal. What's missing? What is the key ingredient or little trick without which the recipe won't turn out right? For a great pie crust, my mom used Crisco and a few drops of cold water. We can teach a brief and effective way to share the Gospel. We can teach people to look for opportunities to share the Gospel in their daily life. We can teach people to defend the faith. However, without a life of sacrifice and service, that gives credibility to the words we speak, that validates our witness in this day and age with the worldview of our culture, people have no reason to take us seriously.

The purpose of this book is to examine the viability of the church given the landscape of religious beliefs and lifestyle in our culture. My contention is that the church has lost its way so badly that it is no longer effective in carrying out its mission. The church has abandoned whatever religious high ground it once held. We are losing whatever moral authority we have left. We have strayed so far from our mission that we barely resemble that which we were created to be. The community of believers is barely recognizable as the called and chosen people of God. Our voice has been muted. Our reputation has been trashed. We have not only become ineffective, we have actually become a stumbling block when our lives aren't characterized by love and service to those in need.

The Christian church has been folded into the generic category of religion or spirituality. In terms of how we live out our concern for others by caring for them and through gifts of charity, there is nothing special or unique about us. What we have been doing is not worthy of notice or deserving of special attention. We are not especially inspiring and do nothing that sets us apart from the rest of society. Others care for the least among us just as well as we do. Recently their charity and philanthropy have reached extraordinary levels. Many of the super-wealthy have taken the "giving pledge."

Apparently, Christ's suffering and death on the cross doesn't mean much to us. We don't seem to be overjoyed. It doesn't appear as if we have been spiritually transformed and are ready and willing to re-order our priorities in a manner that reflects the new meaning and purpose that defines our lives as those who have been bought with a very high price. How else do we explain our tepid response to all that Christ has done for us? If we are to show our love for God by loving our neighbor, then it would certainly appear that we don't love God all that much. We fizzle out on the follow-through. Our efforts are pitiful. We do just enough to give the appearance that we are good people, but we find a way to wiggle out of a life of commitment and surrender that reflects Christ's total commitment to us. Living lives of dedicated service is the exception rather than the rule. It doesn't seem to matter what denomination or congregation we belong to, we all come up short. We all get it wrong when it comes to our response to all that God has done for us.

All the while, the world watches and knows exactly how dedicated we are – or aren't. They don't see love, commitment, and dedication. They don't respect us. They don't look to us for spiritual leadership. They aren't inspired to follow. We shoot ourselves in the foot. They look at how we live and don't want anything to do with Christianity.

The number one issue facing the church today is our lack of credibility due to our failure to walk the walk and back up our teachings about how much God loves us with a response of dedicated service. We are spiritually bankrupt. Our anemic response has been a poor witness to the world. Nobody sits up and takes notice: "Hey, just look at the dedication and commitment and love of those church people. We sure can't say that they are hypocrites. They really care! They are for real!" While doing good works, including the giving of alms, tithes, and offerings is taught, our response can be described as poor at best. In truth, our track record has been a disgrace. We have become spiritually impotent and are in a steep decline.

In a recent Bible class, a parent opened up and shared his heart. "Several of my kids have left the church. I don't see them much; they now live away from here. If I said something about going to church, they would resent my interference and the 'distance' between us would increase. They wouldn't want to talk with me. How do I handle this?" Many Christian parents express similar thoughts. They will say, "We did everything you said, everything you taught us to do, everything we knew to do, everything possible, but we are not getting through; we are losing our kids. Where did we go wrong?"

Certainly the issue is multi-faceted and complicated. When we sort through all of it, what we come up with is that how we express and live out our faith has a greater impact on our children's spiritual formation than anything else. If our kids reach a point where they are struggling with their faith, where they have some doubts and are experiencing hurt, and then they see us living out a partial, compromised version of Christianity, they are likely to continue questioning and could drift away from a walk with the Lord. Alan Lull, a man of faith, who is a Lay Minister and Director of Youth and Missions at St. John's Lutheran Church in West Bend, Wisconsin says: "God doesn't seem real to our young people because He isn't real in the lives of their parents." This is a clue about what this book is about. Those who do not know Christ see us the same way that our kids do. They are not impressed. They are not inspired. They see no reason to follow.

The Church On Life Supprt

So here's where we've come so far. The Church is in decline. The "foolishness" of what we preach is certainly a stumbling block. However, the main reason for not being effective witnesses is our failure to walk the path of compassion and service. The world hardly notices us because we give an uninspiring witness. We don't make a very good impression on our kids or those we hope to reach with the Gospel because we aren't living as sacrificial servants. What accounts for our not being sacrificial servants and ultimately led to the decline of the church is what the next four chapters are about.

My intent is to bring all of this out into the open where we can all struggle with it together. There are factors that influence our faith and life that we aren't aware of. These spiritual blinders are a huge part of the reason why we have come to the place in the church today. My purpose in writing is to encourage prayer, study, and reflection about a church that is deteriorating, decaying, and dying because of a witness that is less than inspiring to those we are trying to reach with the Gospel. We have waffled by teaching an understated and compromised understanding of discipleship, which has resulted in a pitiful witness that inspires no one, and we didn't even realize it. We are up to our ears in the sinfulness of consumerism and materialism and didn't notice. We don't see the big picture.

The church is on life support. Maybe that's overstating it, but maybe not. I really don't expect anything to change. I don't expect Christians to do things much differently. I don't expect us to try to raise the bar more than a little. The church will continue to decline. It is heartbreaking to watch us destroy ourselves.

Chapter 5

"So Tell Me, Exactly What Does a Disciple Look Like?"

The challenge from someone who has been a committed and active Christian servant all her life was, "So tell me, exactly what does a disciple look like?" The church became entangled in the lifestyle of our culture and lost its way when it compromised, and, thereby, redefined "discipleship." The result of our teaching of an incomplete, understated, misleading, and deceptive understanding of discipleship is that Christians no longer understand what a disciple looks like. How can they? We no longer teach it. We don't even come close.

Traveling down the road of life with "basin and towel" in hand and a purse ready to open to help care for those beaten and left by the side of the road is not standard operating procedure for us. Hopefully, explaining the biblical understanding of what it means to be a disciple will be a vehicle for the Holy Spirit, working through the Word, to empower and change our lives to be more closely aligned with the full picture of what it means to be a disciple. Up until now, we've waffled in our teaching. We take one shot at teaching radical discipleship with a bow and arrow in the midst of a battle for our souls that uses modern military technology and equipment. Occasionally, we slip in a zinger, without providing the context and supporting material necessary for clarity. In an 18 minute sermon, or one hour Bible class, it's like we use a laser pointer to highlight a passage or phrase about discipleship in 10 seconds, when what is called for is an extensive explanation. We come out of our bunker, fire one round, and retreat, somehow thinking that we have made our contribution to advancing the mission of the church.

We now live the redefined model of discipleship, and the redefined model of what it means to be a Christian. We give a less than inspiring witness because we don't understand what it means to live out the biblical model of discipleship. Consequently, as others see it, we live pretty much like everybody else. We aren't living out the biblical model of discipleship, in part, because we haven't been taught the biblical model of discipleship. The church lost its way when it inadvertently, unknowingly, and unintentionally became entangled in the expansive web of lifestyle and culture, resulting in adopting and teaching a compromised, incomplete, understated, and therefore, misleading and deceptive understanding of discipleship.

The very definition of the church's mission includes the word "disciple." "Go therefore and make disciples of all nations, [. . .] teaching them to observe all that I have commanded you" (Matthew 28:19, 20). The words "disciple" and "discipleship" occupy a place of primary importance in Christian theology and Christian life. They have now become some of the most misunderstood words in the Christian vocabulary. What we have taught about the meaning of these terms is grossly inadequate. There is a total disconnect between the biblical description of a follower of Christ and what we see in the lives of Christians. The difference between what we teach about the meaning of these words and what the Bible teaches is astonishing, as are the consequences of how this discrepancy has impacted the state of the church today.

We frequently use the words disciple and discipleship when describing the process of teaching people what it means to be a Christian and how that translates into living as one. As long as we continue to teach an incomplete, inadequate, and distorted version of the truths found in the Scriptures, there will be no change in the declining course of Christianity. Our teaching reflects a timidity and cautiousness that stifles commitment and dedication. The growth of the individual Christian is stunted and the process of spiritual maturation is short-circuited. Tragically, the whole Church suffers from this minimalist interpretation.

However, once the issue surfaces, once Christians become aware of it, once they begin to get the drift, once they are challenged with the whole enchilada, some want to know more and ask, "Tell me, exactly what does a disciple look like?" The person who asked me is someone I know well. She graduated from a Lutheran High School, has been active in church using her many gifts as a volunteer, and who continues in Bible study. Their small group Bible study had been wrestling with that question for several years. While they studied various books of the Bible and various topics, their discussions would often circle back to the same question, "Tell me, exactly what does a disciple look like?" My sense is that she and her group are not alone.

Here is what I consider to be a biblical explanation of discipleship. After we become a Christian, discipleship involves our whole self and everything in our life. Discipleship includes worship, Bible study, sacrificial service, involvement in mission, stewardship (managing all that God has entrusted to our care, time, talents, and treasure), and how we live out our vocation.

Many Christians hold to the notion that having knowledge about Christ is enough to be saved. If they have the knowledge, they're good to go. The Lutheran way of saying it is, "I've been confirmed." But they aren't walking and talking with Him daily in a close, personal relationship, and their life reflects a minimalist understanding of what it means to be a disciple.

Many Christians are outspoken in their opposition to moral degeneracy, the historical critical method of biblical interpretation, secular humanism, and post-modernism. I get it! What I haven't heard is clear teaching about what it means to be a disciple. What is being a disciple all about? What does a disciple look like? In answering these questions, there is a desperate need for clarity and specificity. What is glaring by its absence is an emphasis on teaching biblical discipleship. This has been missing for a long time. We know the particulars of what sin is (usually described during sermons in terms of moral slip-ups), we know that Jesus died for us and that our moral slip-ups are forgiven, but we aren't clear about what it means to be a disciple. We have a fuzzy sense of it. We hear it described it in terms of generalities and principles. But we aren't given the specifics, and consequently don't get it. We need clear teaching that uses specific examples of household budgets and time-management that asks for a sacrifice that validates the faith that we profess with our lips.

Self-Denial and Service: Core Values of Discipleship

When asked what it means to be a disciple, many Christians will answer, "People who are called to follow Christ." We have to follow-up by explaining what it means to follow Christ, what disciples look like, and how they are different. Living Christianity, not just confessing it, is more than going to church every Sunday, and then living pretty much like everybody else during the week. Discipleship is the spiritual equivalent of Obsessive-Compulsive Disorder. We are called to become obsessive-compulsives in yielding ourselves in complete surrender to Christ. It is an eager, willing, and joyful surrender. The call of God, in the Scriptures, is a call to willing obedience, not something we have to do and not a life into which we are dragged kicking and screaming. It is an obedience that is humbly submissive—something we want to do. Discipleship is a way of life consumed with a passion to praise and honor Jesus by loving and serving others in his name. Discipleship is something that happens in the lives of Christians as we come to and are moved by the ever increasing awareness that we are richly blessed.

Discipleship is being a faithful follower of Jesus, who loved us enough to suffer and die on a cross in our place and as our substitute, taking the punishment for all of our sins. He is our King, the One who we want to sit on the throne of our lives. As God's children, knowing what He has done for us, we don't want to do anything that would dirty His name or harm His reputation. We bear the name Christian, and everything we now do is because we want the name of God to be honored. We want to live in a way that does not tarnish God's good name, empty it of significance, or treat it as if it were irrelevant. For the Christian, living to honor God's name becomes a natural thing. It is who we are. It is what living the Christian life is all about.

When others look at us, they need to see God. They need to get an idea of what God is like. God's intention is for people to look at us, and then praise and magnify His name because of what they see in us. God's name is to be lifted up in our lives, so the rest of the world will come to know what an awesome, fantastic, loving God we have.

Some of the Bible passages that describe discipleship and good works lack specificity, yet convey the lofty intent of the radical and all-encompassing nature of a life of sacrifice and service in meeting the needs of the neighbor. Other passages are quite specific. There is no question that our teaching emphasizes the passages which are lofty and inspiring, but which are also quite general. In sermons, we are usually taken to the mountaintop, then sent back down into the plain with an explanation of discipleship which lacks clarity and specificity. We receive little guidance on how to live as Christians in the real world. The beautifully written passages about good works need to be translated into a plain English explanation of the all-encompassing nature of doing good works, and it has to be done with specificity and detail.

Philippians 4:8 is a beautiful passage, one we are inclined to put in the category of that which is at the heart and core of what makes a disciple: "Finally, brothers, whatever is true, whatever is honorable, whatever is just, whatever is pure, whatever is lovely, whatever is commendable, if there is any excellence, if there is anything worthy of praise, think about these things." The disciple is urged to live in harmony with God's will. The disciple's entire life is to bear witness and demonstrate how to live for Christ. This principle is stated in qualities and characteristics that are truly inspiring, but that doesn't mean they are specific. We need to know exactly what a disciple looks like. Am I getting picky? Am I splitting hairs? I don't think so. If we want to understand the essence of what a disciple looks like, we have to be more specific.

Discipleship is an attitude of the heart that compels us to respond to what Christ has done for us with lives of sacrifice and service. As disciples, we are called to commit ourselves to self-giving, self-sacrificing, and selfless lives of love and service. Now, we are starting to get the idea of what a disciple looks like. Disciples are to be a gift to those whom God sends us to serve today. Disciples are deeply concerned about and pray about poverty, suffering, inequality, discrimination, and exploitation, and they are ready to do all in their power to address these issues. Disciples believe that each one of us "has a nearly infinite degree of duty and obligation to the other."[20]

The church looks nothing like what it is supposed to be: a community of saints committed to meeting the needs of "the least of these," including those who face a deck that is stacked against them and a playing field that is not level. George Bernard Shaw reminds us: "The worst sin towards our fellow creatures is not to hate them, but to be indifferent to them; that is the essence of inhumanity."[21] A disciple lives modestly and gives generously in order to best serve the poor, the downtrodden, and the oppressed. Now we are starting to get a better idea of what a disciple looks like. In response to Christ's self-sacrificing love for us, clearly demonstrated on the cross, we joyfully, willingly, and without coercion embrace a life characterized by a singleness of service - to love others as our God has loved us. We stand ready, in complete submission, to serve faithfully until we depart this earthly life.

As Christians, we have so many reasons and so much motivation to be dedicated disciples. It is all rooted in the Gospel. An awe-filled gratitude to the God of the universe, who, even though He didn't have to, expressed His love in sacrificial service by breaking down the barrier of sin that separated us from Him. The Gospel is the "Good News" that our sins are forgiven through the suffering and death of our Lord Jesus Christ, and His rising from the grave on Easter morning with the assurance that we will be able to share in His victory over death and the grave. "For God so loved the world that he gave his one and only Son that whoever believes in him will not perish but have eternal life" (John 3:16, NIV). We are overwhelmed with a love and gratitude that shapes every aspect of our lives. We are transformed and moved to live a life totally devoted to the

One who suffered and died for us. All we do becomes a response to what He has done for us. We are overjoyed and ready to completely surrender ourselves to Him in a life of loving service, commitment, and dedication. This is why we are different! At least this is how it should be.

Once the heart of God is revealed to us and we become aware of the enormity of His love for us, we would think it would make enough of a difference for others to easily see the difference in our lives. Unfortunately, Christian teaching isn't often followed in practice. We aren't transformed into people who want to express our love in lives totally dedicated to His service. Somehow, this part of the message gets tuned out. His call to a life loving service gets shuffled off to the side together with the very real and often desperate needs of others. Martin Luther speaks to the issue. "Those who know and accept the child Jesus also give honor to God but treat their fellow men [. . .] with peaceable demeanor, glad to help [. . .] any man [. . .] where each gladly does the best he can for another."[22]

Luther's continues on this subject:
The apostle Paul said (Phil. 2:5-11), "Let this mind be in you which was also in Christ Jesus, who being on equality with God, emptied himself, taking the form of a servant, and becoming obedient unto death." Paul means that when Christ was fully in the form of God, abounding in all things, so that He had no need of any work or any suffering to be saved, was not puffed up, did not arrogate to himself power, but rather in suffering (abuse at the hands of those who arrested him, enduring the pain of the cross) and dying made himself like other men. [. . .] All this he did to serve us. When God in his sheer mercy and without any merit of mine has given me such unspeakable riches, shall I not then freely, joyously, wholeheartedly, unprompted do everything I know will please him. I give myself as a sort of Christ to my neighbor as Christ gave himself for me.[23]
Being a disciple means being Christ to our neighbor.

Mother Teresa described discipleship in exactly the same way. It is a Christian being Christ to his neighbor. Mother Teresa was concerned about the deprivation and powerlessness of the poor and emphasized the importance of having compassion for the weak. To her, they were Christ. To them, she was Christ. "The dying, the crippled, the mentally ill, the unwanted, the unloved – they are Jesus in disguise."[24] "She would often repeat the question, 'How can you claim to love a God you can't see if you fail to love the brother standing right in front of you.'"[25] Mother Teresa served, labored, and loved in the slums of Calcutta nearly 70 years. She was an inspiration to so many because she represented the best of Christian tradition. She committed herself to living out the twofold commandment to love of God and neighbor. Here was a witness whose words and lifestyle were one. Mother Teresa was the essence of what the Christian life is all about. Her ministry to the poor, sick, and dying is the essence of discipleship.

Her norm was the self-giving, self-sacrificing, selfless life of Christ who gave Himself on the cross for her. She ventured into a world of absolute poverty, surrendering her whole life into the service of her Lord. Her only desire was,

"to dedicate herself to the service of His suffering poor. 'God wants me to give myself to him in absolute poverty [. . .] by tending the poor in the slums, the sick, the dying, the beggars in their dirty holes and the little street children.'" "By absolute poverty I mean real and complete poverty – not starving – but wanting – just only what the real poor have."[26]

This is what a disciple looks like. Self-denial and service are a way of life. When a disciple serves the least favored, oppressed, disadvantaged, alienated, downtrodden, excluded, abandoned, lonely, forgotten, and those on the margins of society, they are serving Jesus. God helps others through us. There is never a blind eye turned to mistreatment and suffering.

We get out of bed in the morning concerned about our job, how we are going to pay the bills, about the quality of the education our children will receive, the tension in our marriage, or about the rebelliousness of our teenager. These are very real issues. However, at the same time, we need to be concerned about those in our country, and throughout the world, who are malnourished, refugees displaced by civil wars, regional conflicts, and threats of violence, parents with sick children who have no access to basic health care, and the homeless. Our personal challenges do not absolve us from our responsibility to also love and care for others. Our personal circumstances are not sufficient grounds to justify a special dispensation that frees us from our responsibility to care for the poor and disadvantaged, or others who are troubled and burdened. This is what discipleship is about. Now we are beginning to get a good idea what a disciple looks like. I offer it as a model that can serve as the baseline for evaluating what it means to live out our faithfulness as disciples.

People often do the extraordinary when faced with a difficult situation – like rescuing someone from a burning car or from high water during a flood. Disciples do the extraordinary thing all the time. Disciples are faithful men and women who, moved by the Holy Spirit working through the Word, repent, that is they are eager to turn their lives around and walk more closely in accordance with God's will and ways.

The Biblical Description of Discipleship: the Sublime and the Specific

When someone wants to know about the heart and core of what a disciple looks like, it is essential that we use passages quoted directly from Scripture. They carry the weight of a description that Scripture has provided. The importance of these Bible passages needs to be emphasized. They are the foundation for all that follows. Want to know what a disciple looks like? Here's the description straight from the Bible. This is what a disciple looks like!

Lofty Passages that Inspire

Matthew 28:19, 20 "Go therefore and make disciples of all nations, [. . .] teaching them to observe all that I have commanded you."

I John 3:11 "For this is the message you heard from the beginning, that we should love one another."

John 15:12 "This is my commandment, that you love one another as I have loved you."

John 13:34, 35 "A new commandment I give to you, that you love one another: just as I have loved you, you are to love one another. By this all people will know that you are my disciples, if you have love for one another."

Matthew 5:16 "Let your light shine before others, that they may see your good works and give glory to your Father who is in heaven."

Luke 6:31 "As you wish that others would do to you, do so to them."

Micah 6:8 (NIV) "To act justly and to love mercy and to walk humbly with your God."

<u>Passages with Enough Specificity to Get Our Attention</u>

Romans 12:1, 2 "I appeal to you therefore, brothers, by the mercies of God, to present your bodies as a living sacrifice, holy and acceptable to God, which is your spiritual worship. Do not be conformed to this world, but be transformed by the renewal of you minds [. . .]."

II Corinthians 5:14, 15 "For Christ's love compels us, because we are convinced that one died for all, and therefore all died. And he died for all that all who live should no long live for themselves, but for him who died for them and was raised again."

Matthew 22:37-39 "You shall love the Lord your God with all your heart and with all your soul and with all your mind. This is the great and first commandment. And a second is like it: You shall love your neighbor as yourself."

Mark 8:34, 35 "And calling the crowd to him with his disciples, he said to them, 'If anyone would come after me, let him deny himself and take up his cross and follow me. For whoever would save his life will lose it, but whoever loses his life for my sake and the gospel's will save it.'"

Matthew 20:25-28 "But Jesus called them to him and said, 'You know that the rulers of the Gentiles lord it over them, and their great ones exercise authority over them. It shall not be so among you. But whoever would be great among you must be your servant, and whoever would be first among you must be your slave, even as Son of Man came not to be served but to serve, and to give his life as a ransom for many.'"

<u>Passages with a Clarity that is Truly Challenging</u>

Matthew 25:37-40 "Then the righteous man will answer him saying, 'Lord, when did we see you hungry and feed you, or thirsty and give you a drink? And when did we see you a stranger and welcome you, or naked and clothe you?' And the King will answer them, 'Truly I say to you, as you did it to one of the least of these my brothers, you did it to me.'"

Luke 10:25-37 "And behold, a lawyer stood up and put him to the test, saying, 'Teacher, what shall I do to inherit eternal life?' He said to him, 'What is written in the law? How do you read it?' And he answered, 'You shall love the Lord your Gods with all your heart and with all your soul and with all your strength and with all your mind, and your neighbor as yourself.' And he said to him, 'You have answered correctly, do this, and you will live.' But he, desiring to justify himself, said to Jesus, 'And who is my neighbor?' Jesus replied, 'A man went down from Jerusalem to Jericho, and he fell among robbers, who stripped him and beat him and departed, leaving him half dead. Now by chance a priest was going down that road, and when he saw him he passed by on the other side. So likewise a Levite, when he came to the place and saw him, passed by on the other side. But a Samaritan, as he journeyed, came to where he was, and when he saw him, he had compassion. He went to him and bound up his wounds, pouring on oil and wine. Then he set him on his own animal and brought him to an inn and took care of him. And the next day he took out two denarii and gave them to the innkeeper, saying, "Take care of him, and whatever more you spend, I will repay you when I come back." Which of these three, do you think, proved to be a neighbor to the man who fell among the robbers?' He said, 'The one who showed him mercy.' And Jesus said to him, 'You go, and do likewise.'"

In order to understand the impact and power of this parable, we need to know the back story. Over a period of about 700 years a long standing and deep-seated hatred developed between Jews and Samaritans. After the fall of Samaria in 722 B.C., many Jews were taken into exile to Assyria. The Samaritans were a people of Jewish heritage who had been left behind. They intermarried with the people brought in to resettle Samaria. In the eyes of Jews, who later returned to Jerusalem, they were regarded as half-breeds, not pure Jews. Yet, after two good Jews passed by the man beaten and left by the side of the road, it was a Samaritan who stopped and helped. How much more applicable could the parable be to the issue of immigration and the unreconciled history of race, ethnicity, and religion? Today's disciple applies the principle and teaching of the Good Samaritan to our culture. This is what a disciple looks like!

James 1:27 "Religion that is pure and undefiled before God, the Father is this: to visit the orphans and widows in their affliction, and to keep oneself unstained from the world."

I John 3:17, 18 "But if anyone has the world's goods and sees his brother in need, yet closes his heart against him, how does the love of God abide in him?"

Luke 12:33 (NIV) "Sell your possessions and give to the poor."

II Corinthians 8:1-4 "We want you to know, brothers, about the grace of God that has been given among the churches of Macedonia, for in a severe test of affliction, their abundance of joy and their extreme poverty have overflowed in a wealth of generosity on their part. For they gave according to their means, as I can testify, and beyond their means, of their own accord, begging us earnestly for the favor of taking part in the relief of the saints [. . .]"

I Timothy 6:6-10 "But godliness with contentment is great gain. For we brought nothing into the world and we can take nothing out of it. But if we have food and clothing, we will be content with that. People who want to get rich fall into temptation and a trap and into many foolish and harmful desires that plunge men into ruin and destruction. For the love of money is the root of all kinds of evil."

The clarity, detail, and preciseness of the clear and challenging passages add considerable meaning and depth to the passages that tend to be more inspirational, general, and global, and the passages that begin to get our attention. Their amplification gives us a much better sense of the powerful message God intends to convey.

When we read all of the passages again, we get it. Now we understand. We have a sense of the fullness of the power of God's message for those who would be His disciples. The power and authority in the booming voice of God is unmistakable. It is like when lightning strikes very close by and the loud clap of thunder follows. I've also been blessed to hear the deafening roar of the waterfalls at Niagara and Yellowstone. Then there was the pitch dark night on the beach in Ventura, California. It was after midnight. Everyone had gone home and the parking lots were empty. There weren't many lights, and those that were there weren't bright. They were also quite a distance from the water. It was a night when the waves were huge, but I couldn't even see them until my feet were almost in the water. That night in Ventura, the deafening roar of the turbulent surf was awesome; it just kept pounding. Each time I now hear God speaking through any of the passages that are part of the call for self-denial and service, it's like experiencing the awesome power of those huge ocean waves breaking on the beach in the dark of the night; God is speaking, loud and clear. This is what it's like for disciples. These passages are God explaining to us what a disciple looks like.

Disciples Surrender, Sacrifice, and Serve

After reaching the point in the development of my thesis where people began to get a sense of what I was writing about, one person responded, "You can't expect us to live like paupers!" That's not what I said, but I know what he meant. The way others express it may be a little different, but the underlying thoughts and feelings are pretty typical. The kind of discipleship I'm describing is not what Christians had in mind when they signed up to join the church. I understand that this response, as well others that are similar, are attempts to deflect the issue so we can avoid the necessity of having to deal with it, and face the truth about ourselves. A pauper is one who is poor and receives charity. I'm not suggesting that we give until we are so poor that we need charity ourselves. However, I am most certainly suggesting a level of self-denial, sacrifice, and frugality that goes way beyond what folks in our culture would consider anywhere near reasonable. Then again, we're not talking about being reasonable. We're talking about being disciples.

What I am saying is that we have to come to terms with, and come to peace with, our answer to the fundamental issue of meaning, namely, what life is all about. We have to ask the fundamental questions about our identity (Who am I?) and purpose (Why am I here?). Disciples stand out in a crowd because they are noticeably different. We will be identified as religious fanatics, but properly understood, that's a good thing.

Jesus lays claim to our entire life, a life characterized by a singleness of purpose, namely, to love and serve others as our God has loved and served us. When we review the Bible passages, there are no terms or conditions, no caveats or contingencies, and no exceptions or exclusions. When discussing this with an acquaintance, he tried to convince me that there were some reasons to be positive and hopeful based on many examples from the lives of people he knew who were really committed to helping others. The question that remains, and that we must respond to, is whether or not we come anywhere near our potential in terms of self-denial and service?

We all have to figure out what to do with this teaching. If the only thing that counts is faith active in love (Gal. 5:6), then my life will no longer be conformed to the world, but it will be transformed into one characterized by sacrifice and service. A Christian whose life cannot be characterized by self-denial and service is a contradiction. Now we are getting a pretty good idea of what a disciple looks like. Discipleship is a call to total submission, surrender, and obedience that follows the example of how the Lord served us. When the breakthrough comes, there is a total change in our orientation toward life.

What the Lord has done for us transforms us, and through the Holy Spirit, we find the strength to proceed beyond our attachment to the world, moving to a transcendent life of service and duty to our neighbor. We commit to living self-sacrificing, self-giving, selfless lives of service for the sake of Him who went all the way to the cross for us. We live in the joy of forgiveness, even for the failures we will experience in our ongoing struggle with living self-centered lives.

Disciples are faithful in daily devotions, meditation, Bible reading, prayer, and introspection about how they are living the Christian life. We are completely devoted to loving God and showing our love for Him by loving our neighbors. We are always on the lookout for opportunities to be involved in ministry in our congregations, community, and the larger church. We want to be involved in service all the time. We want to do what Christ would do in any situation.

Disciples cannot be indifferent. Does that describe us? Are we indifferent? Our self-examination includes reflection on the words of Shaw noted earlier. "The worst sin toward our fellow creatures is not to hate them, but to be indifferent to them, that is the essence of inhumanity."[27] When I heard those words for the first time, it was like a laser piercing the darkness and opening a new window into my soul and the world around us. All we want is to be left alone so we can provide for our families, live respectable lives, and enjoy a little of the good life. Basically, we're good people. Leave us alone. Don't bother us.

However, we can't avoid the truth that we look out not just for the needs of our own but also for their wants, at the expense of the unmet needs of others. The chorus of response is quite predictable. "Come on! Get real! Are you losing it? You want strangers to become as important to me as me and mine? Once our needs are met, you want me to treat strangers in the way I treat my own?" Yes, because God does. This is what a disciple looks like.

Here is a window into our souls. We learn a lot about ourselves when we have to decide where to draw the line that separates responsibility for our own family and indifference to the needs of others. It is at the point where our needs and the needs of our own are satisfied that the choices get tougher; this is when Shaw becomes relevant, as he creates an ethical dilemma of titanic proportion.

As long as we are financially stable and enjoy some of the trappings of the good life, and the American Dream, we settle into a comfort zone where we are quite content. The needs of others living in want, suffering, and misery rarely appear on our list of priorities, let alone at or near the top. Most of the time they aren't even on our radar. The old adage, "Out of sight, out of mind," is an apt description of our attitude. "Indifference" is our middle name. Strangers aren't as important as family!

In the fall of 2017, I received a great book of devotions about stewardship from a friend. It was awesome. If we want to know what a disciple looks like, these are great descriptions!

Nothing is more valuable and commendable, and yet not one duty is less practiced, than that of charity. We often pretend pity and concern for the misery and distress of fellow creatures, but yet seldom commiserate their condition so much as to relieve them according to our abilities. But unless we assist them with what they have need of, for the body, as well as for the soul, all our wishes are no more than words of no value or regard, and are not to be esteemed or regarded; for when we hear of any deplorable circumstance, in which our fellow creatures are involved, be they friends or enemies, it is our duty, as Christians, to assist them to the utmost of our power [. . .].

For if we have not charity, we are not Christians: charity is the great duty of Christians; and where is our Christianity, if we want charity? Therefore, let me beseech you to exercise charity to your distressed fellow creatures. Indeed my dear brethren, this is truly commendable, truly valuable; and therefore, I beseech you in [. . .] tender mercy to Christ, to consider his poor distressed members; exercise, exercise, I beseech you, this charity. If you have no compassion, you are not true disciples of the Lord Jesus Christ. I humbly beg you to consider those who want relief and are really destitute, and relieve them according to your abilities.[28]

"What will it cost me – in terms of time, in money, in effort, in the matter of my friendships?" [. . .] What must our Lord think of us if His work, and His witness depend on the security and the safety and convenience of His people? [. . .] What measure of sacrifice, bother and disturbance is there in your Christian faith? Add sacrifice to your giving by thinking of those less fortunate and sharing some of what you have with them. Add bother to your schedule by carving out more time for prayer and less time for some other activities. Add disturbance to your diet by fasting from something so you can feast on Jesus.[29]

Teach those who are rich in this world not to be proud and not to trust in their money, which is so unreliable. Their trust should be in God, who richly gives all we need for our enjoyment. Tell them to use their money to do good. They should be rich in good works and generous to those in need, always being ready to share with others (I Timothy 6:17-18).

Few people consider themselves 'rich.' However, statistically, most of us in 'developed' countries are 'rich.' [. . .] At least 80% of humans live on less than $10 U.S./day. If we begin with this basis, then we are indeed 'rich.' So what should we do about it? [. . .] Be satisfied with the basic necessities of food, clothing and shelter. Beware of simply wanting what others have or others expect you to have.

Work on getting your security from God, not wealth, and seek to please God in words and actions.[30]

These disciplines (simplicity, stewardship and sacrifice) reinforce each other, since they relate to our attitude and use of the resources that have been placed at our disposal.

The discipline of simplicity or frugality refers to a willingness to abstain from using these resources for our own gratification [. . .].

The related discipline of stewardship encourages us to reflect on our lives as managers of the assets of Another. [. . .]

Sacrifice is a more radical discipline than simplicity in that it involves the occasional risk of giving up something that we would use to meet our needs rather than our wants. This is a faith building exercise that commits us to entrust ourselves to God's care.[31]

We are called to offer "spiritual sacrifices" (I Peter 2:5). Later on in this chapter Peter calls us "a chosen race and a royal priesthood," called out of darkness to declare God's praises. How are you doing at managing the resources that God has given you so that those resources help you declare his praises?[32]

The Rev. Dr. Matthew C. Harrison, president of the LCMS, properly balances forgiveness and faith with ministry and mercy in a way that is most helpful.

Love, care and concern for those in need [. . .] are motivated by the Gospel. [...] Love seeks and serves the neighbor. [. . .] The Gospel gifts bring forgiveness, and beget merciful living. Lives that have received mercy cannot but be merciful toward the neighbor. [. . .] "Repentance ought to produce good fruits [. . .] the greatest possible generosity to the poor" (Apology of the Augsburg Confession 12.175). Christ's mandate and example of love for the whole person remains our supreme example for life in this world and for the care of the needy, body and soul. Christ's Palestinian ministry combined proclamation of forgiveness and acts of mercy, care and healing (Luke 5:17-26). [. . .] In describing the events of the last day, Christ noted the importance of mercy in the life of the church ("as you did it to one of the least of these My brothers, you did it to me [Matt. 25:40].[33]

The emphases I'm lifting up indicate that amplification and clarification of the phrases "cannot but be merciful" and "ought to produce good works" are desperately needed. Otherwise we will continue the confusion and misunderstanding surrounding what it means to be a disciple.

Wiggle-Room

We look to the passages that are more general in nature to carve out the wiggle-room needed to escape the all-encompassing call to obedience. Many passages allow considerable latitude in choosing our response. If we decide to rationalize, justify, and bring them into conformity with our own understanding of Christianity and what the church is about, we can. We prefer the more general ones. We squirm when we hear the passages that are quite specific, such as I John 3:17, 18: "But if anyone has the world's goods and sees his brother in need and closes his heart against him, how does the love of God abide in him?"

We don't seem to be overjoyed, ecstatic, jubilant, or thankful about hearing the portions of the Bible that speak specifically to the Christian's attitude toward this world's goods. If we are, our lives don't show it much, if at all. We like the messages about forgiveness, comfort, encouragement, and support, but how do we feel about the other part of the message? We get cheated when we aren't told the rest of the message, that all of what God has blessed us with transforms us and inspires us to find the fullness of joy by following in the footsteps of the One who sacrificed and served, the One whose love and mercy are incomprehensible and unfathomable. Without both parts, we come away feeling unsatisfied. We know something is missing, and we still haven't found true meaning and purpose in our lives.

We describe discipleship in high sounding terms, we use glowing descriptions, we seek words that are designed to move and inspire, and we often use the awesome words of Scripture to do so. Then we stop – "full stop." We don't go on and provide the detail - the specifics that make it crystal clear. At that point, we let our hearers and learners off the hook. We give them an out. We give them more than enough wiggle room to avoid having to examine themselves in terms of how well we fit the job description.

Asking the hearer to figure out for themselves how these passages apply to their lives is a "cop-out" of the highest order. Assuming that they will follow through is just so patently unrealistic. Sinners tend to deal only with what they have to. We are not going to start looking for ways in which we are not living as disciples – that is expecting way too much from us. With few exceptions, it has to be spelled out for us, or we won't be able to connect the dots.

As Eugene Peterson explains, while God's will is not difficult to understand, we teach it in a way that allows for uncertainty. We allow our people to jump right into the void, always trying to carve out some wiggle room.

An excellent way to test people's values is to observe what we do when we don't have to do anything, how we spend our leisure time, how we spend our extra money. [. . .] Will we let God be as he is, majestic and holy, vast and wondrous, or will we always be trying to whittle him down to the size of our small minds, insist on confining him within the boundaries we are comfortable with, refuse to think of him other than in images that are convenient to our lifestyle? But then we are not dealing with the God of creation and with the Christ of the Cross, but with a dime-store reproduction of something made in our image. [. . .] Not only do we need to let God be God as he really is, but we need to start doing the things for which he made us. We take a certain route; we follow certain directions; we do specified things. There are ethical standards to follow, there are moral values to foster, there is social justice to pursue. [. . .] None of it is difficult to understand. [34]

Discipleship - Selling Out for Christ

Christians who are living in obedience to God's law devote themselves to trying to love God and neighbor more completely. Disciples care for the poor and comfort the afflicted, even when it involves a sacrificial drain on our resources and energy. This is what we are called to do. This is what discipleship is about.

Discipleship is an invitation to break from cultural norms. Discipleship is a call into a life of dedicated service, where we find ourselves moved by the Holy Spirit to a place where true meaning is found, a life where we will find the abundance of joy, healing, comfort, peace, meaning, and purpose.

We are transformed into the lifelines that God is throwing out to others who are in desperate spiritual and physical need. Discipleship is a life of sacrifice and service where we become God's witnesses to those who have not yet found Him and what it means to have a full and abundant life.

Churches often use any burden of guilt over past sin, and broken relationships and the messes that result from those sins as an entry point for membership. The invitation of God often goes out to those who are experiencing grief, loss, trials, troubles, heartbreak, loneliness, and hardship. People whose lives are coming apart are desperately searching for hope, healing, and peace, and want to find an answer. Our invitation is to join the church, and find peace and healing. This isn't a bad thing, but it is a sad thing when we don't include the call to a life of self-denial and service. It can become counterfeit Christianity, if, after there is healing, we don't explain discipleship in terms of selling out for Christ.

Discipleship is a life of willing obedience and loving service. We are no longer being conformed to the world's thinking, but, rather, we find in Jesus our reason for being and purpose in living. Discipleship is following the "new commandment I give to you, that you love one another: just as I have loved you, you are to love one another" (John 13:34). Discipleship is having a burning passion for lost souls and a burning passion for those Jesus called "the least of these" (Matthew 25:40) - the disadvantaged, the underdog, the rag-a-muffins, those suffering injustice, and the poorest of the poor.

Discipleship is selling out for Christ. Discipleship is a commitment to live according to God's plan, not our own. Discipleship is seeking to get on the same page with Him and help to accomplish His agenda. The disciple understands that living the life we want to live and having our own plans, hopes, goals, and dreams, and asking God to get with the program and help make it happen will only lead to emptiness and disillusionment. Discipleship is finding the joy in living that comes when we are humbly and joyfully obedient to our Lord and Savior. Discipleship is having Jesus at the center of our life. Discipleship is when Jesus is our reason for being. Discipleship is when Jesus is our everything. Discipleship is when we believe that Jesus gave His all for us, and in grateful devotion, we seek to give our all back to Him in service. This is what discipleship is all about.

Christ has no body but yours,
No hands, no feet on earth but yours,
You are the eyes with which he looks with compassion on this world,
Yours are the feet with which he walks to do good,
Yours are the hands, with which he blesses all the world.
    Teresa of Avila (1515-1582)

After worship one Sunday, an unbeliever, brought to church by a friend, said, "If I believed what the pastor said, and what you say you believe, my life would be transformed, and everybody around me would know it." Amen! All of this sounds like a foreign language to most Christians. Only a few, a very few, "understand."

Some great Christians to talk to about what a disciple looks like are Mother Teresa's Sisters of Mercy. They tell us that when our basic needs are met, meaning in life is found in helping others, especially those who lack the basics: food, shelter, and medical care. What we will not hear from them is a claim of goodness, let alone sainthood.

Mother Teresa had great sympathy for those who felt rejected and unwanted: the forgotten parents left in an old people's home, the lonely youth whose family did not care [. . .]. You know, there are many people all around us who need to be cared for. "Having taken Christ's words 'Love one another as I have loved you,' and made them a reality in her life, she invites us to travel along the same path [. . .]. Starting by loving the unloved, the unwanted, the lonely closest to us in our homes, communities, and neighborhoods, we can follow her example of loving until it hurts, of doing always a little more than we feel ready to do. [35]

On the other hand, she was also well aware of her humanity and began her journey afraid of how it might become a roadblock to fulfilling her commitment.

I am so afraid Jesus—I am so terribly afraid—let me not be deceived—I am so afraid.—I am afraid of the suffering that will come—through leading that Indian life—clothing like them, eating like them, sleeping like them—living with them and never having anything my way. How much comfort has taken possession of my heart.[36]

The way she saw herself and the words she uses to describe herself are striking. "My own Jesus—what you ask it is beyond me."[37]

Mother Teresa isn't the only well-known exemplary disciple in the history of the church. "Origen of Alexandria, (c.185 – c.154) abandoned temporal comforts in service to the church."[38] Before 325, "all Christians more or less lived an ascetic life,"[39] exercising their Christian faith in a strict manner that included prayer, fasting, and almsgiving. They stood in stark contrast to the society around them. Born into a wealthy family, Francis of Assisi "renounced [. . .] finance and took up a life of humble service. [. . .] imitating Christ through voluntary poverty and service. The three vows of poverty, chastity and obedience were taken as marks of the ideal Christian servant."[40] Zwingli (1484-1531) taught that only "a radical shift in one's life" [41] was acceptable to God. "Ximenes de Cisneros (1436-1517) . . . encouraged a higher spiritual life (by) all the clergy and laity alike."[42] "Pietism had its roots in the context of a spiritual awakening in Lutheranism and other religious groups in the seventeenth century."[43] Inspired by Charles Spurgeon, William Booth established the Salvation Army in 1865. "Their program of spiritual and social action" (reached out to) "the poor, the homeless, the destitute (and) the outcasts of society."[44] Adolph von Harnack (1841-1930) encouraged believers to "practice humility through love."[45] During the turbulent 1960's the World Council of Churches expressed concern about poverty, world hunger and service. Pope Francis VI (2013-   ) is "a strong advocate for the poor and the oppressed . . . and (often clearly restates his) commitment to social justice."[46]

There is no question that implicit in discipleship is a preferential option for the poor. Here is the way Mother Teresa put it. "There are plenty of nuns to look after the rich and the well to do people—but for My very poor, there are absolutely none. For them I long—them I love."[47]

Chapter 6

A Simple Life

Disciples understand what being a follower of Jesus is all about and don't get offended when they hear the call to self-denial, sacrifice, simplicity, and frugality. They "get it!" They know what is being asked of them. They welcome the reminders of those who hold them accountable. A disciple is a good manager of the resources with which he has been blessed. Therefore, the influence of changing cultural attitudes about accumulating "stuff" that began after World War II, when the economy grew to the point where many more of us were able to have a share of the American Dream, presented us with a huge challenge. Along with the opportunity to accumulate a lot more wealth came new ethical, moral, and religious questions about how to use it. As it relates to creature comforts, what is God-honoring and what is not?

So, what does a disciple look like in terms of the stewardship of our financial resources, especially when it's possible to pursue our wants rather than just our needs? What does our struggle with a call to commitment that involves self-denial and service look like in our lives? This awareness brings out a number of common responses, questions and concerns. Is it wrong to pursue a share of the "American Dream? Surely it's ok to buy as nice a home as we can afford, and upgrade when able? Aren't we entitled to some nice vacations? Can't we spend a little more than we need when we go out and eat?

The desire to accumulate more stuff is an extremely powerful motivation. We've totally underestimated its influence on the lives of disciples. After WWII, the American Dream was broadly realized in the middle-class. It was assumed that if we were honest and worked hard, it was there for the taking. We had the opportunity to improve ourselves economically on a scale never before possible in the history of the world. This became one of the bedrock values of what life in America is all about.

The pursuit of the American Dream became a driving force in lower-class and middle-class families. Church members, along with others, wanted to accumulate as much wealth as possible for themselves. We, too, were dazzled and distracted by the possibility of accumulating considerable wealth and enjoying a whole new lifestyle.

Where do the clergy and church leaders fit into these developments? They were very dedicated people, content to live on modest means, and thankful for the small increases in salary the growing economy made possible. What they didn't realize, however, was that much more mission, evangelism, outreach, and service could be accomplished, if they challenged their people to practice sacrificial, first-fruits giving with their additional income. By the time everybody figured all of this out, it was too late. Church members saw the American Dream as something in which they, too, could have a share, and they became accustomed to the good life.

While members won't say it directly to the preacher, we can be sure of what they're thinking, and what they're saying in the parking lot or in the car on the way home. "It's my money. I've worked hard for it. It's nobody's business what I give." Those who have unfortunately grown up with a totally distorted impression of church might even say, "The preacher better keep his grubby little hands off my wallet." For those who are trying to be faithful, this issue presents us with a huge challenge. We get really touchy when someone tries to tell us what to do with our money. We don't want anybody asking for sacrifices that would put a crimp in our lifestyle. When we perceive that the church is sticking its nose in where it doesn't belong, we don't like it. When the church comments on our personal business, we get defensive.

We aren't all that excited about being a member of a church that teaches sacrifice or self-denial. We don't want to hear that. Unfortunately, to our spiritual detriment, we didn't hear about it either. Since we didn't hear about the hidden temptations and dangers found in the pursuit of materialism, the good life, and the American Dream, it was easy to get caught up in it together with everybody else. These were good times in America. The middle-class grew and enjoyed having a share of the American Dream. This was the way it was. We were all caught up in it. Understandably, only a few of the clergy were able to step back and gain a perspective of the big picture. A major cultural shift had occurred. The shift would continue to go unnoticed and its impact on the church was bigger than anyone could imagine. We as clergy and leaders didn't realize the need to preach and teach about it.

The issue is further complicated by the widely held perception of life as a daily grind for middle class Americans. No one is saying that life is easy. Most of us work hard to support our families. However, most of us enjoy a modest lifestyle.

Most Americans Live Paycheck-to Paycheck - No matter how much you earn, getting by is still a struggle for most people. Seventy-eight percent of full-time workers said they live paycheck-to-paycheck, up from 75% last year, according to a recent report from Career Builder. Overall, 71% of all U.S. workers said they're in debt. While 46% said their debt is manageable, 56% said they were in over their heads.[48]

However, we have to keep in mind that this is only half the story. What we don't know is how well they managed their finances while they were going into debt.

What we do know is that Americans believe they are entitled to a share of the American Dream. We have an economy where "many people in working-class jobs have a higher standard of living than most people have ever had throughout history. (At the same time an) estimated 20,000 to 30,000 children [. . .] die every day (every day) of starvation or diseases related to malnutrition – diseases that could have been prevented."[49] "Half the world's people live on less than $2 a day and a billion people on less than $1 a day [. . .]."[50] If we in the Christian community had provided food, shelter, and health care, we could have made a difference. Millions are destitute: they live in a condition of extreme need without the necessities of life. Here in the U.S., "In 2015 there were 43.1 million people in poverty. [...] 19.4 million Americans live in extreme poverty. This means their families cash income is less than half the poverty line, or about $10,000 a year for a family of four. They represent 6.1 percent of all people and 45 percent of those in poverty."[51] Sadly, as Grant Mc Govern wrote in a letter to the Journal Sentinel titled "A 'me' Society," "most [. . .] of society's members spend their lives taking care of themselves instead of one another."[52]

Finding Excuses for Not Responding to Human Need

To figure out exactly what a disciple looks, like we need to answer another question: What does evil look like in our lives? The evil inherent in our human nature is implicit in phrases like "the survival of the fittest," "every man for himself," and "looking out for #1." We have this innate tendency to look out not just for the needs of ourselves and our own, but also for our wants, at the expense of the unmet needs of others, many of whom are living in misery and despair. It's our nature to find excuses for not responding to those in need. We experience a powerful internal tension between lives that are self-centered, self-seeking, and self-serving on the one hand, and self-giving, self-sacrificing, and selfless on the other. This gets to the heart and core of what our human nature is really like. It includes everything that is implied when we use the terms "self-interest" and "greed."

While our human nature hasn't changed over the years, what has changed is a tremendous increase in income along with the opportunity to spend it on the things, recreation, and pleasures that are part of the "good life." We simply have more ways for our nature to express itself. So, it's harder than ever to walk faithfully as a disciple.

Through the use of a distorted, even tortured, evangelical logic of discipleship, we have adopted an image of ourselves as decent people who have occasional lapses in character, making only relatively minor incursions into the realm of the immoral and unethical, and who demonstrate a level of greed and self-interest that is inconsequential. The truth is that we are rotten to the core. Our lives are characterized by the relentless pursuit for more. It doesn't seem that we ever have enough. Greed and self-interest are operative principles, rather than sacrifice and service. We make choices and decisions that demonstrate we are almost oblivious to the plight of others.

We rationalize, reframe, and reconstruct reality the way we want life to be, rather than seeing life the way God sees it and living life His way. There is a huge gap between how we see ourselves and how God sees us, also between how we behave and how we think we behave. God sees us one way, and we see ourselves totally differently. We fail to see just how much misery could be alleviated and how much suffering could be relieved, if only we were more concerned about the unmet needs of others. A disciple is one who seeks the help and strength of the Holy Spirit to constantly fight against the evil inclinations of our human nature.

Providing for those in our household is our responsibility and the right thing to do. Yet, we experience a constant moral and ethical tension. We have to ask if it is being cold, insensitive, and indifferent, when somebody else's child is starving to death, and we do nothing about it, even though we could? Is it the right thing to do to make sure my kids have a decent place to live? But how "decent" becomes an issue when the toilet drains through the neighborhood of another child's house, and we could have done something about it. Is it cruel and inhumane when somebody else's child has malaria, dysentery, or AIDS through no fault of their own, and our family could do something to help, but doesn't? Within the context of our own financial resources and the choices we make in pursuit of the American Dream, do we ponder and pray about how our decisions impact others? As we make decisions within the framework and circumstances of our lives, we have to consider whether or not we are disciples.

Are we kind when our children and grandchildren have much more than they need, and we quickly forget the anguish of parents whose hearts are aching because they can't provide enough food, clean water, or basic health care for their children? Are we disciples when we consider excessive spending in the context of looking on as anguished parents hold their kids while they starve to death? Are we kind when our kids are given too much, and we spend too much on music lessons and music camps or athletics and club sports, while the children of other parents are facing bitter and hopeless poverty, disease, hunger, or even starvation, and have almost no hope of receiving health care or getting an education? Can such behavior really be described as being the caring, kind, loving response of a disciple? This isn't how God wanted it to be. He hoped His disciples would have responded differently to His self-sacrificing love shown on the cross. The literal meaning of compassion is to spill out our guts in order to help others; this is discipleship.

Most of us see ourselves as decent, neighborly, law abiding citizens who believe that, "basically, we're good people." "We're good Christians." Maybe we're civilized and decent, but thinking that we are good is at best a delusion. Most of us don't come close to being kind, caring, and compassionate. How can we be so calloused as to think we can spend our time and money any way we want, when there are so many in our world who are starving and in desperate need without the modest hope of being able to live in dignity and safety? If we don't say it, we act like it is every man for himself. If we don't admit it, we act as if our organizing principle is the survival of the fittest. The truth is, we are, indeed, self-centered, self-serving, self-seeking folk who look out not just for the needs, but also for the wants of ourselves and our own, at the expense of the unmet needs of others.

The American Dream describes the aspirations of prosperity and well-being for the average person. It is framed within a context where there is an opportunity to move up the economic ladder. The cherished American notion is that we are an opportunity society, where the hope of upward mobility is there for us all. It is up to us to go for it. We may not have much today, but as long as there's a chance to move up the economic ladder, it's all good. We want our children to live better than we did. In the process, we acquire an appetite for more and a higher standard of living.

We have been deceived by the lifestyle of our culture, the American Dream, and the "good life." We become preoccupied with our needs and demonstrate lovelessness toward our fellow man, while coming up with all kinds of ways to rationalize no more than token responses to the needs of others.

The recent history of the Church in the United States has been written within the framework of living in the heyday of the American Dream, a sweet spot in our economic development, resulting from a once in history alignment of population, industrialization, globalization, and technology. We have been deceived by the cultural definition of success, the "good life," and the American Dream. Resisting the attraction of "the good life" is a huge challenge with human nature being what it is. A middle-class lifestyle in the US has such an appeal, and yet, it does not fit within the biblical understanding of discipleship. Therein lies the tension.

Beyond Generosity

Discipleship goes beyond generosity; it is a call to sacrifice. In II Corinthians 8 and 9, we find the heartwarming and inspiring story of congregations in Macedonia who gave out of their own extreme poverty to those who had even less. During an offering for the less well-off church in Jerusalem, their joy in the Lord moved them to give generously even though they themselves were extremely poor. In II Corinthians 8:2-5, Paul gives us a clear and unmistakable picture of what a life of discipleship looks like.

> In a severe test of their affliction, their abundance of joy and their extreme poverty have overflowed in a wealth of generosity on their part. For they gave . . . beyond their means, of their own accord, begging us earnestly for the favor of taking part in the relief of the saints – and this, not as we expected, but they gave themselves first to the Lord and then by the will of God to us.

When describing discipleship, we are going beyond generosity, to the point where we give in a manner consistent with the principle practiced by the Christians in Macedonia. Poverty didn't hinder their generosity. They pleaded for an opportunity to give.

The foundation of everything Paul teaches about giving is grace, "the unmerited favor, the undeserved love, that God has given and continues to give to his people. God's grace is a giving grace; it centers around his gift of Jesus Christ and his redemptive work on our behalf. That grace moves the Christian to be gracious – to freely, gladly give everything, including his material goods, back to the Lord."[53]

"They had offered back their whole selves to the Lord who had offered his Son into death for them".[54] II Corinthians 8:9 says, "For you know the grace of our Lord Jesus Christ, that though he was rich, yet for your sakes he became poor, so that you through his poverty might become rich." "The offerings a Christian brings are a fruit of faith, the response of a grateful heart to the goodness of God."[55] "The grace, or unmerited love, of God that brings salvation to the sinner also inspires a new life of service that includes unselfish, generous giving. [...] [When] apprised of the plight of their sisters and brothers in Jerusalem [. . .] they could not help but give."[56] If we want to know what a life of discipleship as a follower of Christ looks like, here we have it.

Here is what the ascetic lifestyle would look like today. The operative principles of self-denial and service would be expressed in a lifestyle that is modest, simple, and frugal. While not advocating a call to the asceticism of St. Francis of Assisi, we definitely need to lean strongly in that direction. It is a model that, with revision, could be very helpful for those who choose the path of discipleship. One of the ladies in our small group home Bible study said, "You want us to be little Mother Teresas, don't you?" I responded, "Somethin' like that." She heard what I was saying, and she was on the right track. She was on the track that brings joy, satisfaction, meaning, and purpose for all of us.

Many point to Mother Teresa as an exception to the rule. The implication is that there is no way we can be expected to be like her. Why should Mother Teresa be an exception? We could adopt the same guiding principles in our lives. Most people I talk to react with statements like these: "You've got to be kidding." "You can't expect us to be like her!" "That is too idealistic!" "You're out of touch with reality." "You're a dreamer." Implicit in these assertions is that we have a right to more of this world's goods than she had. Our assumption, however, is neither correct nor Christian. Our lives need to characterized by simplicity and frugality. The higher and more noble purpose in life is to choose a life-style of self-denial motivated by a concern for, and a desire to better meet the needs of, our brothers and sisters in the human family. We seek to be self-giving, self-sacrificing, and selfless, rather than self-centered, self-serving, and self-seeking.

Sacrificial living and sacrificial giving, in our time, can hardly be compared with the hardships borne by the ascetics. We need to carefully reflect on the standards and guidelines that are appropriate for us in this time and in this place. I am most definitely advocating for the consideration of a lifestyle based on the principles of self-denial and loving service that are essential for those on the journey of spiritual maturity. All of us continue to resist owning the truth about ourselves as believers, who in the calculus of indifference are more culpable than unbelievers by an exponentially larger factor. Traveling down the road of life, ready to care for those left for dead by the side of the road, is not standard operating procedure for us.

Contentment

An essential part of the Christian life includes living modestly, giving generously, and serving faithfully. Biblical teaching is clear: God never intended that we have it all. To the degree we are blessed, we are called out to help those in need. We are our brother's keeper. It's tough to deny ourselves when others in the culture and in the church are not making similar sacrifices. Materialism and a consumer mentality permeate our culture.

Where do we draw the line when it comes to choices about big screen TVs, iPhones, designer clothes for the kids, computers, music systems, music lessons, athletics, and how much we spend on vacations? It isn't easy, as we are tempted to want as much as our neighbor. Our culture tells us that it is not just o.k. to strive for what others have, it's downright American. It stimulates the economy and creates more jobs.

Some have been gifted by God in a way that leads to success and making a lot of money. Fantastic! Take care of our needs, then give the rest away. I can already hear the response: "Excuse me! Run that past me again." There is nothing wrong with being able to earn a lot of money. What I hope is that those who have been touched by God's love and whose gift is making money will use it for the well-being of others.

But godliness with contentment is great gain. For we brought nothing into the world and we can take nothing out of it. But if we have food and clothing, we will be content with that. People who want to get rich fall into temptation and a trap and into many foolish and harmful desires that plunge men into ruin and destruction. For the love of money is the root of all kinds of evil (I Timothy 6:6-10).

We want to be comforted by the assurance of forgiveness for our sin. We want to be comforted in our sorrows. We would like to have at least some creature comforts. As disciples, however, we are also concerned about the spiritual and physical needs of others. The very purpose of our lives is to show our love for God by making service to others our number one priority. A disciple is a good steward. He lives frugally and is a good manager of the resources with which he has been blessed. Discipleship is the antithesis of acquiring things and amassing possessions. When disciples have more of the world's goods than we need, we make every effort to use the excess to help meet the unmet needs of others. We have to find a way to address this issue with members and those considering membership. It has to be covered thoroughly. We can't just avoid the issue.

Budgets ~ The Nitty-Gritty of Discipleship

Psalm 24:1 and Psalm 89:11 teach that everything belongs to God. God doesn't transfer ownership to us. It's all His! It is not ours to do with as we wish. We are stewards of what God has entrusted to our care. We always ask what God would have us to do with it. Now we'll get into the specifics of what it means to live modestly, simply, and frugally, so we can use the rest to serve others.

Passionate stewardship sermons based on Scripture, but lacking in specifics, are not all that helpful. They do us a disservice. They make it easy to duck the gravity of the issue by cloaking it in generalities. They allow more than enough wiggle room for us to find a way to avoid having to really struggle with these teachings and do some soul searching. We use the excuse that we have to be cautious when deciding what the standard should be. While this issue needs to be approached with care and caution, we can't use this as an excuse to avoid addressing it directly and thoroughly. It seems to me that there is another reason why we don't want to be specific. There is a fear that it would be flat out rejected by congregational members who don't want anyone getting so deep into the nitty-gritty that they can't avoid the truth that they aren't giving enough.

There certainly are faithful men and women who, moved by the Holy Spirit working through the Word, repent and are eager to reform their lives and walk more closely in accordance with God's will and ways. The Word touches their hearts, and they want to live it. Here's the kicker! They don't know how. They don't know what it means to live it. They need help to learn how to live out their desire to be faithful. They need the specifics. We all need to hear what a disciple practicing Christin stewardship looks like. We need as thorough and complete of a description as possible.

We'll focus directly on the decisions we have to make as individuals and families, given our vision of the American Dream. This is where the rubber meets the road. How can I do right by my spouse and kids, while not forgetting about the welfare of others? When purchasing food, clothing, shelter, and vehicles, can we spend frugally? How do we differentiate between needs and wants? Where does concern for the needs of the poor and needy fit into the picture? Obviously, we don't need a Rolex or a Rolls Royce, but, exactly, what does get included?

After prayerfully seeking the guidance of the Holy Spirit, Christian stewards make intentional decisions about every line item in their budget. These are examples of the questions we need to ask.

Food – When we go out to eat, will we spend more than we need to?

Lodging – Should we purchase a bigger residence than we need? How much do we spend on furnishings?

Clothing – What's unnecessarily expensive?

Vehicles – What vehicle and options meet our needs for functionality and safety, rather than luxury?

Electronics – What smart phones, iPads, computers, and flat screen TV's are sufficient to meet our needs?

Entertainment, Recreation and Vacations – How much should we allow for: Recreational vehicles, including choice of campers, motor homes, boats, trailers, snowmobiles, etc.? Vacation homes and timeshares? Vacations, including how much to spend and how many to take? Sports tickets, concert tickets, movies, and the arts?

Kids Activities – How much shall we spend on athletics, music lessons, and dance?

Retirement – Can we do some of the things we've always wanted while we have the time and resources?

Estate Plan –How will we direct the distribution of any financial assets that remain after we go to heaven?

The vision of the American Dream appeals to all of us. We all struggle with it. These are choices we make in the midst of a really powerful internal struggle. Are the decisions we make consistent with the stewardship of what God has entrusted to our care?

"Ouch! You mean we really have to include all of this in the discussion?" Yeah, and it is not easy. All of this needs to be considered. We must get to this point in order to move forward. It is at the very heart of what this book is all about. For Christians, choices about what to purchase come under the umbrella of the One who gave His all when He sacrificed His life on the cross in order that we can have the guarantee of forgiveness and the assurance of eternal life. His sacrifice is the guiding principle for us as managers of our financial resources. Disciples are good stewards and managers who are modest, frugal, and avoid buying that which is unnecessary. What are some questions to ask when trying to live simply?

Should we buy a car for $37,000 when we can get one that will work just as well for $27,000, or even less?

Can we justify the purchase of new vehicle when the current odometer reads 160,000, and all it needs is a tune-up, tires, front shocks, and brakes to be able to run for another 80,000?

Do we have to eat at high end restaurants? Should we eat at home more often?

Do we spend $3,000 per person to go on a vacation every other year, or should we go less frequently and find less expensive vacations?

What issues are involved in deciding whether to buy a travel trailer? Is it going to be the way we plan to spend most our leisure time, or will it remain parked much of the time?

How do we choose to meet our need for housing?

What will we spend on leisure time activities? Do we choose one more expensive activity, or several that are less expensive?

What about bucket lists? Are we using them as cover to rationalize and justify expenses for travel and vacations in a way that doesn't reflect our responsibility as a sacrificial first-fruits givers?

When making stewardship decisions, we need to keep in mind that many of those to whom the church preaches the Gospel, in the context of the American Dream, are people of modest means. They are people who have to work hard just to make ends meet for their family, are excited just to be able to go fishing for one or two weekends a year, are blessed to be able to go camping or to a cabin for a family vacation, and have to work hard to save several years to be able to afford a small, pop-up camper.

We don't make the connection between aspiring to move up the economic ladder, on the one hand, and, living modestly, on the other. We forget that the road to heaven passes through the poorest neighborhoods in our cities and towns, and the neighborhoods of the millions of the forgotten, marginalized, and abandoned, who have fallen by the wayside.

We don't disagree with what the Scriptures teach in general terms about a God-honoring offering in response to all that He has entrusted to our care. We do, however, interpret this issue differently. Forgetting the destitute and those living in deplorable circumstances that we pass by on our pilgrim journey makes us just like the religious leaders Jesus addressed in the parable of the Good Samaritan, who passed by on the other side.

Believing that "It's all His," how we manage and spend the dollars entrusted to our care is very important. The allocation of income for our residence, vehicle, vacations, recreational vehicles, eating-out, as well as our investments, retirement plan, and estate plan clearly reflect our priorities. How we spend is a reliable barometer of our values and what we believe. Disciples want to do that which is God-pleasing, while resisting the influence of society and culture.

I appeal to you therefore, brothers, by the mercies of God, to present your bodies as a living sacrifice, holy and acceptable to God, which is your spiritual worship. Do not be conformed to this world, but be transformed by the renewal of your mind, that by testing you may discern what is the will of God, what is good and acceptable and perfect. (Romans 12:1, 2)

The seductiveness of our entitlement to the "good life" has influenced us so much that we are basically insensitive to the needs of others; this puts us squarely in conflict with our faith. The physical and spiritual needs of others are of such magnitude that we can't just set them aside, but that's exactly what happens, and in the process, we deny what we say we believe.

We may even give a tithe back to God to help do His work. Even this doesn't necessarily mean that we are sacrificial first-fruits givers. Being a disciple can be much more. It is managing all that He has entrusted to our care in a way that helps to accomplish His work – the mission He has given us. For many with modest means, tithing can be a considerable challenge and inspiring sacrifice. Yet, tithing is not the goal for everyone. Being a hard working middle-class, sacrificial, firsts-fruits giver may mean joyfully and willingly sacrificing to be able to give a double tithe. Those who are blessed to receive a larger income may give much more. At the time of the Great Awakening, a Presbyterian preacher named Charles Finney met Arthur and Lewis Tappan, men who already contributed generously to benevolent associations.

Finney urged them on to greater efforts in philanthropy. 'The world is full of poverty and desolation, and death; hundreds of millions are perishing, body and soul [. . .] God calls on you to exert yourself as a steward, for their salvation; to use all the property in your possession [. . .]' Inspired, the Tappans and their friends formally engaged to give away all their profits, putting aside only what they needed to support their families.[57]

John Kieschnick, Senior Pastor of Gloria Dei Lutheran Church in Houston, Texas, shares a lesson he has learned from helping Christians experience God's love, forgiveness, and strength.

We give out of hearts that overflow with gratitude for God's great grace. If we've experienced even a taste of his love, forgiveness and strength, we won't grouse about giving. Instead, we'll be thrilled to participate with God in his great work. [. . .] Grasping the fact that God owns it all helps me open my hand and present to him all that he has given to me. I tell him, "Here, Lord. All this is yours. What do you want me to do with it?" That prayer is a far cry from daydreaming all day about more . . . stuff! And knowing that God owns it all helps me when I'm shopping because I realize that many of the things I buy, I just don't need at all. That money could be used much more powerfully in other ways.[58]

Don't get me wrong. There is nothing inherently wrong, evil, or immoral with material things or the ways God has provided for our rest and recreation. All of them are intended as blessings. The challenge is to find the proper balance. We forget that, by the standards of the world community, we are rich. We don't realize that our decision making has been influenced by the promise of America and the opportunity to pursue a share of the American Dream. Given the culture, we can easily lose our moral compass and the ability to decide the difference between needs and wants. The danger of being too attached to the things of this world is very real. "No servant can serve two masters, for either he will hate the one and love the other, or he will be devoted to one and despise the other. You cannot serve God and money" (Luke 16:13).

The materialism inherent in our consumer-driven economy makes it tough to be a Christian and make these choices in our culture, but that is exactly what we are called to do. Those with less income have to struggle with whether a small fishing boat and a week's vacation on a lake each year is enough. Those with more income have to make choices about how much to spend on their home, what kind of vehicle to buy, and whether they need a couple of jet skis or snowmobiles, or a vacation home. What is the God honoring way to manage what's His in the way that best helps accomplish the work that he has given us to do? When called to make these tough choices, we need the Holy Spirit's guidance and strength.

What does a disciple look like? There are very real choices with which a disciple has to struggle. There are choices to be made at all income levels. Living at, or slightly above, the poverty line isn't easy, and the spiritual struggle is looking around and seeing others who have much more than we do, and trying to be generous. Most of us on easy street are not grateful for all that we do have, as we always want some of the stuff enjoyed by others who have more. For some, the challenge is to be a sacrificial first fruits giver even though we can barely afford our house payment. We have to decide whether we need the bigger house, a bigger boat, a better snowmobile or a nice vacation every year or two. Disciples really struggle with decisions like these, calling on the Holy Spirit to enlighten and empower. This is what a disciple looks like.

What about those of us who want our children to have a great education. Being as expensive as it is, those of us whose children don't get substantial scholarship aid have to give very prayerful and careful consideration to the cost of a college education. Can we adjust sacrificial, first-fruits giving during the years we incur educational expenses? Some of us are blessed to be in a position where we could help with our kids educational expenses by supplementing what they earn and any student loans or scholarships they get. Later, we could, over and above what we are currently giving to church and charity, make an annual thank-offering equal to the average yearly amount we spent on education. This is the way disciples think. This is the way we look at it! These are the kinds of things disciples do!

Pulling all of these issues together, we then set our priorities and put together a family budget. Blessed abundantly, we have many decisions to make, always holding up before us biblical teaching about what it means to be a disciple who exercises good stewardship. Do we want a nicer home, and then as a trade-off, spend less on vehicles and vacations? Since we like to travel and spend many weekends and vacations in our camper, do we decide that we will spend less on our primary residence? The same kinds of choices present themselves for those whose family priority is a great boat for water sports and fishing, a motor home, or extensive travel. It comes down to decisions about houses and cars, how much we spend eating out and how much we spend on clothes, entertainment, and recreation. These are the conversations that disciples have with God in prayer and with the other members of their household. How much should we allocate for smart phones and data plans? Are we willing to make do with less expensive electronics and clothing, and less recreation and entertainment in order to give priority to becoming sacrificial first fruits givers? It all boils down to this, the Scriptures call us to live modestly and give generously. This is how we practice good stewardship and give a powerful witness.

Accomplishing that objective is a struggle when we don't see others making similar sacrifices. The materialistic, consumer mentality of our culture is inconsistent with the Christian ethic. Most of us are part of a middle-class America that enjoys the good life: a decent home, two vehicles, maybe a pick-up truck, recreational vehicle, boat, snowmobile, four-wheeler or camper. We live quite comfortably and don't hurt for anything. We have to ask ourselves whether we are indifferent to the plight of those burdened by misery and need. In the Bible, it was the orphans and the widows. Today's orphans and widows are single moms with few resources, kids needing foster care or an adoptive parent, the starving, refugees, and those living in poverty.

The indifference of the masses is not going to change, but Christians can. Disciples can. We can be different. While others have convinced themselves that their current lifestyle is one of high ethical standard, it doesn't mean it's true, or that it justifies our living the same way. Most have the mantra: "we've worked hard for it, we've earned it, and we deserve it." We need to remember that it is God who has blessed us with the health and energy to be able to work hard. God has blessed us with more than we need, and we sure don't deserve it. We are so grateful and so thankful. We want to be good managers of what is His – what He has entrusted to our care.

While in the process of writing, I came upon this in one of my daily devotional readings. "Jesus calls us to grow into stewardship maturity by living more simply. Eternal rewards are not found in bank accounts and the accumulation of so-called toys. The one who dies with the most toys wins . . . nothing! They do not desire or expect all of the other material stuff available in our economy."[59] Disciples are thankful just to have the basics.

"Retired" Disciples

Even those of us who have retired from our daily vocation have to be honest with ourselves about the choices we make as disciples. Here are two very different pictures of what retirement might look like.

Vision one goes like this. Is there a place where I can volunteer in my congregation or one of its ministry arms? Are there any elderly or homebound who would be blessed by regular weekly or monthly visits? Finding a place where I can have a meaningful volunteer experience in my community would also be very important to me. It would be such a blessing to be part of a good Bible study, and a small group where we discuss the challenges we are facing in life, and the issues of the day. I would like to try to start a summer camp or year round reading group for kids achieving at below grade level; their parents would also be invited. I look forward to having some time to read, spend on my hobby, and take a little vacation once in a while. Frosting on the cake would be heading south for a vacation on the gulf coast, or in Florida, Texas, or Arizona for two weeks every third winter, going to New York to see a couple of Broadway plays, or visiting some of our great national parks.

Here is vision two. We'll see to it that we get to church every week, and when in town we'll sign up to help out at church dinners or be responsible for the coffee and rolls on Sunday. We've worked hard for years, and now we have time to play a lot of golf and go somewhere warm for a couple of months in the winter. There are so many places we want to visit. We'd like to go on a cruise once in a while and get to New York and take in Broadway play a couple of times a year. The point is, there are important choices to make. This is serious stuff. This is where it gets real. We need to take all of this to the Lord in prayer big time. These decisions reflect who we are as disciples.

A disciple who is a sacrificial, first-fruits giver lives frugally, is a good manager of the resources with which he has been blessed, and needs an estate plan that directs the distribution of whatever resources remain when they die. Here are a few possibilities for how a disciple thinks about an estate plan. Funds that were set aside for residential care, but not needed, could be designated for distribution to church or charity. A will or trust can also stipulate how the excess funds can be used in our family for the education of future generations. Yet, it is really difficult to know whether future generations will make good decisions and use the gifts responsibly. Would a disciple designate that these funds be distributed to church or charity instead?

These are choices that disciples prayerfully and carefully consider, and issues with which we all have to wrestle. A disciple's decisions are informed and guided by their relationship with a loving God, who sent His Son to be our Savior - a Son who lived the self-giving, self-sacrificing, selfless life of a servant. The items on our bucket lists reflect our priorities, and define what we perceive to be a life well lived. It identifies the source and essence of the contentment, satisfaction, and completeness needed to have a sense of closure about our life.

Only the Bare Necessities

Some would say that this discussion doesn't go far enough. Catholic Bishop Thomas J. Gumbleton says, "If you really want to challenge people, tell them they don't have a right to what is beyond their needs when others lack the barest necessities."[60] This is where it gets really uncomfortable. This is radical! Then again, what's so radical about it? It sounds like what's taught in the Bible. Has the Bible deserted us, or have we deserted the Bible? There are some hard conversations we have to have with ourselves and with the Lord. What really knocks our socks off is that He loves us so much that God sent His Son to die for us on a cross so our sins are forgiven, and He is ready to listen. He's ready to have that conversation with us.

I'm not advocating that, like the ascetics, we give away all of our possessions, but we need to move far closer to that end of the continuum than we have ever considered. I am most certainly saying that we have a whole lot to learn about living frugally and modestly. I am saying that there is a need to begin a radical transformation in the ethics, morals, and values that determine our lifestyle. God wants us to manage all of His gifts in a manner that many would label fanatical. We should consider others as being as important as ourselves. We, who have the world's goods, should not close our hearts to those in need. Are we ready to make sacrifices? Are we willing give away that which is more than we need?

Listen to Kieschnick again.
> Have you ever seen pictures of starving people in a Third World country and thought, "How sad. Too bad we can't do much of anything about it." But is it true that we're helpless to meet that need? A fascinating article about John and Sylvia Ronsvalles, the founders of *Empty Tomb, Inc.* in Champaign, Illinois, tracked consumption and giving patterns of Americans and American Christians in light of desperate needs around the world. In "The State of Church Giving Through 2003," the Ronsvalles assert, "If members of historically Christian congregations in the U.S. had given at the 10% level in 2003, there would have been an additional $156 billion available. The potential impact of this additional money is seen in the need statistics that could be addressed in Jesus name: $5 billion could stop the majority of 29,000 deaths a day around the globe among children under

5, most of whom are dying from preventable poverty conditions; $7 billion could provide basic education for the world's children.[61]

I find these statistics to be astounding, and especially so in light of Jesus comments that "as you have done it for the least of these my brothers, you have done it for me" (Matthew 25:40, RSV).

Kieschnick continues:
> Too often, we excuse our selfishness and blind our eyes from the needs of others. We think, "Hey, I deserve everything I've got"[. . .] Or "I've worked hard for my money. I'm sure not going to give it away!" [...] You and I are incredibly wealthy. "Well, no," some of us might be tempted to say. "I don't have a boat like Frank, or a new car like Janice, or a big house like the Marshalls." If we compare ourselves with the next level up the economic ladder, we'll always feel disappointed and sorry for ourselves. . . . Middle-class Americans enjoy a standard of living that would be the envy of the wealthiest people in the world only a couple of generations ago, and the envy of most of the world today. If you're going to compare, look through the eyes of gratitude and truth, not envy and demands.[62]

Being richly blessed with the resources to have a nice home and vehicle, and enjoy recreation, travel and entertainment, or even have a vacation home, isn't reason to assume that we are entitled to all of it. Rather, it means that God has placed us in the upper management of the stewardship of what is His.

Much of our good fortune is the result of being blessed by God to be born in the time between the 1940's and the present, a period of unprecedented economic growth. The wealth of the masses in our country is unmatched in the history of the world. How blessed we are to have born at this time of fantastic advances in health care and an economy that has the potential for all to be beneficiaries of the wonders of healing, and a level of wealth that was unimaginable for many centuries. How blessed we are to have been born at this time. It's not that we have forgotten how blessed we are, we aren't even aware of it. We don't realize what the world was like just a few short years ago. Therefore, our response is not inexplicable. We simply have never realized how blessed we are. We take it for granted. In this context, our response makes perfect sense. We have hardly scratched the surface of what it means to give thanks to God. For Christians, reaching the goal of tithing is a big deal, and we continue to find great joy, as with the help of the Holy Spirit, we move forward to the next step of double or triple tithing. For those who do not believe, a big deal is going to a concert that benefits charity or making a contribution to an on-line fund-raising campaign.

What's a Need and What's a Want?

The challenge is to define the difference between needs and wants in the context of our consumer-driven, materialistic culture. It's tough given that our decision making as consumers reflects sophisticated marketing techniques intended to manipulate and influence our choices. We don't think about how rich we are, in part, because we have been brainwashed into thinking that the essence of the promise of America is the opportunity to pursue the American Dream. In the process, it is easy to abandon our moral compass and the ability to distinguish between needs and wants.

Who decides between what's a need and what's a want? The Christian ethic provides an excellent baseline to guide the process of searching for an answer. Distinguishing needs and wants from a Christian perspective means remembering all Christ has done for us, our brothers and sisters in the human family who are in desperate need, the very comfortable lives we live, and the biblical cautions about being too attached to material things.

The amount of worldly goods possessed by many is light years beyond what anyone could have ever imagined just 100 years ago. The level of affluence is far greater that anything they could have dreamed. The potential for sacrificial giving far exceeds what it used to be. Therefore, what is called for is a "no beating around the bush" style. There can be no mincing words. We have to tell it like it is. In the context of what Christ has given and sacrificed for us, God's message to us today has to be quite

challenging, much more so than anything we are hearing in
When we start squawking, when we start complaining
understanding of discipleship is far too demanding and unrᴄᴀᴌᴵꜱᴛᴵᴄ and
needs to be toned down, we need to pray about it and be encouraged to just
be with it, and let the Holy Spirit do His thing through the Word. When
teaching about discipleship, the church has indeed been complicit in a
conspiracy to perpetuate mediocrity, and in doing so, has lost its soul.

We have allowed the prevailing attitudes in the culture, and in the
church, to influence our thinking about charity, good deeds, good works,
compassion, and sacrifice. In the process, we have disregarded biblical
teaching when defining good works and discipleship in a culture where
affluence is enjoyed by a larger portion of the population than ever before.
The challenge for all of us as Christian stewards and disciples is to find
balance between "the good life," a nice house, vehicles, smart phones,
computers, a recreational vehicle, and nice vacations with sacrificial, first-
fruits contributions to church and charity.

The founder of Chick-Fil-A, S. Truitt Cathy, said, "I'm not driven to
make money. I am called to help others through my business endeavors,
through my giving, and by the very fact that my service centers provide
jobs."[63] He got it! Making money is certainly not a bad thing. If making
money is our gift, we need to make all we can. Then, give it away to those
in need and to help spread the Gospel.

While having breakfast at McDonald's, one of the regulars asked what I
was writing about. I gave him a quick summary, with emphasis on this
chapter. His response was typical. "You have to remember that we've got
family. We have a daughter who isn't making much in a career in social
services and still has considerable college debt. My wife wants to help her
pay off her loan and do stuff like that." Would his response be consistent
with Christian discipleship? It certainly would, if their own practice of
Christian stewardship had been a witness to her, if she had been
responsible while incurring the debt, and if she has been managing wisely
in order to pay down the debt. It is a spiritual struggle. How can we do
right by our kids and still not forget the welfare of others?

According to Scripture, having it all is not consistent with being a disciple, nor does having quite a bit. The specifics I have shared provide markers that will hopefully be helpful in finding a God-honoring balance. As disciples, we are still a work in progress. By what standard are we measuring what it means to be a disciple? Do we choose the standard? Do we use the generally agreed upon partial, incomplete, and adulterated norm for being a disciple? It seems that we have a greatly inflated sense of our own goodness. We may be charitable enough to be able to salve our own consciences and rationalize that we meet the societal norms necessary for being able to see ourselves as good people. While we may be civilized, decent, hard-working, and law abiding, that is a long way from being compassionate, kind, and caring.

We may even be numbered among those who would help someone in need by giving them the proverbial shirt off our back, but what about the millions of others who need a shirt? What about the millions of others who are starving to death? What about the millions of others dying because they have no medical care? What about the millions of parents who are watching their children die? It is one thing to give someone the shirt off our back and quite another to be sacrificially compassionate.

When reading one of our denomination's theological journals, the intellect and scholarship of the authors of the articles was evident, as was their commitment to our Lord. Conspicuous by its absence was the lack of specificity that accompanied phrases like "lives of faith," "Christian living," "Christ-centered living," and "faithful witness to God's goodness and grace." We're left to connect the dots and to figure out for ourselves the meaning of phrases like these. Another phrase expressed "concern for and solidarity with suffering neighbors." In the context of the culture of our denomination, the words grabbed my attention only because of what I read into them, or, rather, what I have to read into them in order to make them meaningful. In essence, what we do is little more than window dressing. There is little commitment to the principle.

Then, there was one more very catchy turn of a phrase that caught my attention: "See how Jesus heals and restores lives where no one else wants to show up." I liked it. It really resonated with me. I liked the way it sounded. It conveyed a lofty, uplifting vision that I prayed would be followed with action. However, like much of what we have passed off as discipleship, I suspect it was mostly hype. There was no real substance. There were no specifics. Discipleship was this vague and familiar apparition. My evaluation of the article is that it was an articulate description of an entity that is no more than a spiritual hologram. The discipleship it described lacked the substance needed to make it the real deal. So much of what we pass off as teaching about discipleship is more like a page of dots that we need to connect for ourselves, only there are no numbers for us to follow. The way I read what's going on in our circles is that we haven't "shown up" all that much. Eloquent rhetoric isn't matched by a disaster relief plan for lives that need to be restored. All the while, we somehow maintain the belief that we are kind, caring, generous folk who live by the "Golden Rule." All of this just hasn't been raised up clearly enough. We've been given a pass.

"Pope Francis said people 'often make due' [with having] 'health, a little money and a bit of entertainment.' He urged people to help the poor and others in need of assistance, giving freely without expecting anything in return."[64] We have to dramatically increase our efforts to address the needs of the destitute, weak, dependent, forgotten, broken, and the "welfare mom" – all who are experiencing bitter and hopeless poverty. Somehow, we have to break the cycle of poverty, and we, as Christians, need to be in the forefront of that effort. The Church needs to help pick up the slack where government social programs leave off. We, as Christians, seek out those who fall through the cracks. Kids in poor families need a chance. If they come from a conflict-habituated environment and for whatever reasons are not successful in school, they will just perpetuate the welfare cycle. Of course, we need to help with food pantries, housing, homelessness, and jobs. We also try to be sure everyone has adequate child care, transportation, education (for children, youth, and adults), job training, and employment services. Living a life of self-denial and service, we will do all we can to meet the needs of those who are suffering, abandoned, and destitute.

Renounced and respected Christian writer C.S. Lewis echoes the same sentiments.

Charity – giving to the poor – is an essential part of Christian morality: in the [. . .] parable of the sheep and the goats it seems to be the point on which everything turns. Some people nowadays say that charity ought to be unnecessary and that instead of giving to the poor we ought to be producing a society in which there were no poor to which we need to give. They may be quite right in saying we ought to produce this kind of society. But if anyone thinks that, as a consequence, you can stop giving in the meantime, then he has parted company with all Christian morality.[65]

Like others in our society, many Christians also resist looking at it this way. "We worked long and hard to earn a living and raise our family. We did it! So can they!" "We still aren't living the American Dream." "We still aren't enjoying that much of the 'good life.'" "Why should we be supporting them? All they do is use their food stamps for junk food and lay around and enjoy their *iPhones* and big-screen TV's." We resist supporting anything that looks like welfare or the social safety net. When push comes to shove, most of the time the only thing that counts is, "What's in it for me?" Will it help me be able to claim my fair share of the American Dream?

If we are looking for excuses not to give, there are plenty of them, including mismanagement by the recipient organization or foreign governments that have done little to invest in their own development, and instead, spend vast sums on weapons. Then, there are corrupt foreign leaders who fraudulently divert aid into secret foreign accounts. The question is whether these issues become an excuse not to give or a time to re-allocate those dollars to charities in which we have confidence that our contributions will be put to good use. We can always find an excuse not to give.

Several generations have now grown up during a period of upward mobility and increasing wealth. It's a whole new ballgame. We have an abundance of resources with which to support outreach, mission, and charity. Then reality snuffs out any spark or hope that much will change. Christians have been influenced by a culture that prioritizes building a better world for ourselves over building a better one for others. How are we handling the pressure of the temptation? My hope is that the specifics that were shared will be helpful in developing a set of guidelines and principles we can use to do some soul searching and evaluate ourselves as managers of all that God has entrusted to our care.

If someone has never had discipleship spelled out for them, and has never been challenged to a life of surrender, self-denial, and service, or if we have never been called out to live modestly and give generously, that's one thing. Once someone lays it out there for us, that's another. Some people get really upset. Most Christians react something like this: "Describing what a disciple looks like in general terms is helpful. I can handle that. But what you're suggesting is getting a little too close. Actually, it's way over the line in any church where I want to be a member."

Chapter 7

All in Good Time

Christian stewardship also includes the wise management of our time. We just happened to visit a congregation on a Sunday when they distributed a four page chart that included a list of organizations and activities where volunteers were needed, a description of the specific tasks involved and any skills needed, the times when people were needed, and contact information. It was well done. I was pleasantly surprised and impressed. It's really neat when churches compile and organize that kind of information for ministry in their congregations and communities.

It was also a pleasant surprise when I first learned that Jerry Falwell's Thomas Road Church emphasized the importance of being a volunteer. The Thomas Road church:

> was a center of activity all week long. It had ministries for children, young people, adults, elderly people, and the deaf. [. . . It had] a ministry for divorced people and another for unmarried young adults. Each ministry offered programs and activities, including Bible study classes, lectures, trips, sports outings and picnics. They also organized groups of volunteers to visit hospitals, nursing homes, and prisons and to proselytize the community. The organization was so comprehensive that Thomas Road members, old or young, could spend all of their free time in church or church-related activities, and some did just that.[66]

Most of us have the potential to be using much more of our time as volunteers. Sure, many have their hands full earning a living, raising a family, or caring for an aging parent. Yet, it is important for all of us to figure out how much of what fills our days involves choices and preferences that are essential. It seems to me that almost everyone could do so much more as a volunteer servant.

The cultural consensus about what is appropriate in terms of time we set aside to volunteer is so low. Less than half don't volunteer at all. We just don't want to be inconvenienced or make sacrifices. We have an inflated sense of the true level of our concern and compassion for the needs of others. The attitude of the culture is contagious, and many Christians have been effected. It appears as if most us feel that we are already overwhelmed and just don't have time.

Find Out: Do a Time Study

Making improvements in workplace efficiency often involves a time study. In the same way, in order to evaluate how well we use our time as disciples, we have to have data on which to base our conclusions. Why do we need to be efficient and not waste time? Our call to share the Gospel with those who do not yet know Jesus, and to serve those in need, is far too important to approach casually. We need to be careful, structured, responsible, and disciplined. Therefore, keeping a log and charting the use of our time is extremely important. We have to be aware of how we have been using our time by establishing baseline readings.

Monitoring, logging, and charting is very helpful in giving a realistic picture of how we use our time, and can be a real eye-opener. It provides a sense of the overall mix and balance of how our time is used. It also helps us identify our priorities and identify tendencies and preferences of which we are totally unaware. It can help shatter assumptions about a number of our perceptions. The goal for the disciple is to find the proper balance between all of the responsibilities and needs that compete for our time and to develop a plan for how we can prioritize tasks and activities. What gets included, and what will I have to sacrifice?

This is where it gets dicey. We don't want anybody making demands on our time, or suggesting voluntary limitations on recreation and leisure.

We consider it an intrusion into our personal life. The scriptural understanding of the stewardship of time on this side of heaven includes a schedule. What happens now is just as important as eternity. We have time now that can be used to share the Gospel and to serve and help others.

The chart that follows will help us keep track of our use of time. Some may think it is unnecessary. It has been suggested to me that it should be referenced and included as an appendix. My reason for including it is that it is too easy to just put it off and never get to it. Also, it's too easy to assume that we're already too busy. The question is too busy with what?

Here is a suggested list of activities for column one to help in personalizing our study.

Worship, Devotions, and Bible Study

Relationships with Spouse and Children.

Vocation – job, student

Social Interaction – Time with relatives and friends, including, phone time, texts, Tweets, emails, Facebook, and Snapchat

Exercise/Fitness

Volunteer Time

Entertainment, Recreation, Leisure, Travel, and Vacations - reading and watching TV, playing video games, or surfing the web, baseball, basketball, golf, bowling, tennis, and gardening, sewing, crafting, knitting, quilting, ceramics, and cooking movies, concerts, and the arts, camping, boating, snowmobiling, vacationing in an RV, timeshare, cabin, or 2nd home, playing cards and games, and doing puzzles

Activity	Su	Mo	Tu	We	Th	Fr	Sa	Weekly Totals	Total for the Month
									notes:

Activity	Su	Mo	Tu	We	Th	Fr	Sa	Weekly Totals	Total for the Month
									notes:

Activity	Su	Mo	Tu	We	Th	Fr	Sa	Weekly Totals	Total for the Month
									notes:

Activity	Su	Mo	Tu	We	Th	Fr	Sa	Weekly Totals	Total for the Month
									notes:

The stewardship of time is just as important as the stewardship of our financial resources. Most don't pay too much attention to it, because we don't recognize its potential for Christian service. Therefore, it is important to carefully evaluate the use of our volunteer time using specific metrics and a meaningful self-assessment that provides a measure of specificity. While it might seem silly and unnecessary, logging and charting the use of our time by category is so helpful in tracking and evaluating the use of our time in order to get a clear picture of how much time we take for ourselves, compared to how much time we make for meeting the needs of others.

Volunteer Opportunities Abound

Volunteers are valued partners in any non-profit organization. In choosing where to volunteer, we consider our gifts, skills, and areas of interest. We can start by contacting our church and community organizations. Hometown and local newspapers often list volunteer opportunities. The possibilities abound. People are needed to help those from preschool through adult levels with tutoring, reading, and computer training. Handy guys can start people on the path to being carpenters, plumbers, electricians, or auto mechanics. Support staff are needed at shelters for victims of domestic abuse, runaways, pregnant women, unwed mothers, the homeless, and victims of sex trafficking. The poor and needy in our communities can be served by helping at food pantries and soup kitchens or with clothing distribution and at rescue missions. We can work with Habitat for Humanity. We can join church or Red Cross teams that are trained and ready to help with support services and the clean-up following a disaster. Care facilities seek out volunteers to play cards and games with the residents. Some may have the gift of visiting in prisons or working with organizations that help locate jobs for those who have been released from prison. Others may be able to help the unemployed or disadvantaged start a business: lawn care, landscaping and snow removal, home care for the elderly, homebound and disabled, an auto repair shop, or house cleaning service.

There are all kinds of opportunities in which to get involved as a volunteer. There are countless people who need us at veterans' homes, care facilities for the aging, and in big-brother and big-sister programs. There are community and faith-based ministries just waiting for us. Whatever time we have and whatever our physical limitations, there are all kinds of ways we can use our talents and skills to be a blessing to one of these organizations and to give witness to the Gospel.

Evaluating Our Use of Volunteer Time

Disciples want to use their time wisely. The logging and charting of the use of our time by category gives us a picture that can be quite revealing. The objective is that we find the proper balance between our covenant responsibilities as spouses and parents, time for rest, recreation and renewal, and volunteer service in our church and community.

We need time for golf or tennis, woodworking or gardening, knitting or sewing, hunting or fishing, hiking or climbing, biking or camping, ceramics or wood carving, and TV or the movies. For Christians, these activities provide the opportunity for re-creation, refreshment, and renewal, preparing us to return to our primary mission. We always keep our focus on the meaning of our life as disciples, who show our love for God by loving others and helping to meet their spiritual and physical needs. We thoroughly enjoy our leisure time, but it is not what we live for.

Spending a total of 35 – 40 hours a week watching TV, reading, sewing, knitting, working in the garden, playing cards, or golfing, but only two to four hours a week as a volunteer doesn't cut it in terms of coming anywhere near what it means to be a caring and compassionate person. A huge majority have never been challenged to think about it this way. If not, this may be an opportunity to do some soul-searching about what it's like to live a full life, a life of meaning and purpose. Some will say, "It's none of your business, so quit sticking your nose in where it doesn't belong." We have, once again, approached the sinful core of the struggle about what it means to be a disciple.

It would seem that if we spend two hours a day watching TV, two hours a day on our iPhone or computer, play dart-ball or basketball one evening a week, and go fishing once a month on a weekend, with no time set aside for volunteer service, that the stewardship of our time is totally out of balance. If our typical daily routine includes an hour of reading, an hour in the garden and two hours watching TV, with little time set aside for volunteer service each week, then the stewardship of our time is way out of balance. If we watch an hour or two of TV several times a week and volunteer only an hour or two a month, then the stewardship of our time is way out of balance. Spending two hours a day sewing or doing ceramics, a half hour a day reading the paper, and a couple of hours watching TV, with only an hour or two set aside for volunteer service each month, then the stewardship of our time is way out of balance. Spending ten hours a week enjoying our hobby or ten hours a week playing video games, together with a couple of hours watching TV or on our computer and one hour a month volunteering would seem to be quite out of balance for a disciple. Certainly, we can take a week's fishing trip to Canada, go deer hunting or on a golf outing, or vacation with the family in Yellowstone or Disney World. Disciples track all of this carefully and maintain a God-honoring balance.

There is a risk that I am belaboring the issue and turning people off. However, after giving this matter prayerful consideration, it is clear that it is a risk that has to be taken. We have been allowed too much wiggle room in deciding for ourselves what it means to be a disciple. It is too easy for us to rationalize and justify current patterns of behavior. Many examples of the specifics are needed in order to plant the seeds of what the Scriptures teach. It's up to the Holy Spirit to touch our hearts with the Gospel and bring about the growth.

The same goes for retired seniors who are Christians. They certainly need their rest and recreation, chatting and holding court over morning coffee, but the bunch that gathers at their favorite spot for coffee and conversation also needs to track how their time is spent the rest of the day so they too can set aside an appropriate amount of time for caring and kindness. Disciples know they are not just there to be served, but to serve to the degree that it's physically possible. They could be welcomed guests at nursing homes, VA hospitals, or veterans homes, especially when visiting residents who don't get many or even any visitors. Senior disciples who have worked hard all their life know that retirement is not just about kicking back, taking it easy, and doing all of things we always wanted to do and still can. It's about that, but it's also about so much more.

Retirees have so much to offer, yet have opted for bingo, golf courses, early-bird specials, and yard sales. Sure, they've worked hard their entire lives, but how satisfying can it be when the big decision of the day is choosing between a large frozen yogurt or a small one, deciding whether to get a $4.00 "double-stack" or the chicken tender special at Wendy's, or to get some exercise by walking around the mall or by the lake. Some consider retiring early while they still have some money and the time to do what they want. Being a volunteer servant is not usually one of the priorities. With our maturity, skills, and experience, we can become a powerful force of volunteers. We have so much untapped potential to help so many.

Those who garden, sew, or read see themselves as good people. Yet, there are many who are in a world of hurt out there beyond the craft room, workshop, or yard, and many of the faithful do not try all that much to do something about it. We need to be stretched by the Gospel the same way quilters stretch a quilt on a rack. It is one thing to be a decent person, a good neighbor, and upstanding member of the community, and quite another to be a caring, compassionate, self-sacrificing servant of those in need.

We can even spend too much time praying and studying the Bible. Yes, we can study the Bible too much. We have to find the right balance between praying and studying the Bible and putting its teaching into action in loving service. Just being faithful with Bible reading, Bible study, and devotions is not enough. Eventually, it has to translate into service in an active life of discipleship. What about establishing a guideline for ourselves, like three hours of devotions and Bible study need to be balanced by three hours of service? We can't allow ourselves to think that the time spent studying foundational biblical teaching is a substitute for the time needed to show our love for God by loving others in a life of sacrificial service.

If there is a window of opportunity to make significant steps forward in our business or profession, as good stewards, we need to take the time to make the most of those opportunities, even if they require an extraordinary allocation of time. We remain aware that we have made a choice to establish ourselves and our family financially while we have the opportunity, with the intent that at some point it will be clear that we will really get involved as a volunteer.

The time available to participate as a volunteer varies at different points in our lives. Yet, if we're working and our child is involved in club sports and other activities, it is still important to carve out time to volunteer. Having our kids involved in club sports, school sports, and other extracurricular activities may mean that we have to temporarily give up some of the time we spend watching TV, on social media, participating in recreational activities on weekends, traveling, and on vacation. It is also very important for our kids to see us volunteering and for them to volunteer with us.

Finally, don't worry about finding a place that needs us. There are organizations where, in addition to indicating what openings they currently have, are open to considering our gifts, skills, and interests, and see if they can identify a task that meets their needs. We just need to remember that it is their mission, and they know what they need. While it may take a little effort, we should be able to find one that is a good fit. If necessary, they will provide training. There is a place that needs us.

Volunteerism becomes compassion when it remains our priority during the part of our day that comes after we've worked hard to support our family. It becomes compassion when it remains our priority during the part of our day that comes after we have fulfilled our commitments as a spouse, parent, child, relative, and friend. It becomes compassion when it remains our priority during that part of the day that comes after we have exercised and taken time to be renewed, re-energized, and recreated by doing whatever it is that we enjoy, or that allows time to just veg out. Our compassion, as a disciple, can fundamentally change someone's life.

Christian Time-Management

The portrait of a disciple is a person just like us, who is seeking the help of the Holy Spirit to be Jesus' servant presence in the world. For Christians, a big part of life is serving at the soup kitchen or women's shelter. Life is tutoring and mentoring disadvantaged kids or visiting the lonely and aging. Life is taking the blind to the symphony and pushing those confined to a wheel chair through the park. Life is adopting a hard to place child or being foster parents to children whose dysfunctional families are trying to get it together. It is also about listening to the war stories of our veterans and the 'poor stories' of those who are aging. Life is finding beds, mattresses, or a kitchen set or sofa for those who live in bare apartments and sleep, eat, and sit on the floor. Life is doing all we can to see that all people live in dignity.

Life is spending an hour listening to someone who is so narrow-minded and opinionated that everybody else tunes them out or avoids them. Life is spending a half-hour a week reading the Bible, well known hymns, and spiritual songs to someone in the early stages of Alzheimer's or dementia. Life is talking with one of the ragamuffins in our congregation or community who nobody pays attention to or cares about. This is what Jesus did for us. He gave His all on the cross for us. We are honored, eager, and privileged to do for others what He did and to do it in His Name.

The full understanding of service and good works becomes apparent now that we have unpacked the specifics of what a disciple looks like. The challenge for disciples is to make sacrifices in the amount of time we are involved in other daily activities so we can spend more time in service. At the close of the day, we will find quiet and peace, leaving all that is undone in the hands of our heavenly Father until we arise renewed, refreshed, and joyfully ready to greet the new day in anticipation of once again being His love and presence to those He would have us serve that day.

Many will laugh at those of us who give and serve sacrificially. They will think we are suckers. We consider it a privilege. We gladly and willingly adopt a self-giving, self-sacrificing, selfless lifestyle reflected in the stewardship of our time, talents, and treasure. We want to be challenged and strengthened by God's Word in our pursuit of Christian maturity. We ask for the wisdom to be able to discern the difference between needs and wants. For most of us, however, our charitable giving is just a fraction of what it could be, and our volunteer efforts don't come close to realizing our potential. While most really don't want to hear one more sermon about almsgiving, offerings, tithing, sacrificial first-fruits giving, and volunteer service, disciples do.

My hope is that the specifics shared in this chapter and the last will be helpful in developing a set of guidelines and principles we can use to do some soul searching, review our performance as managers, and evaluate the use of our time. We need to be clear about how well we are responding to the call and challenge to live modestly, give generously, and serve faithfully. We can no longer say that we haven't had discipleship spelled out for us clearly and unambiguously, and haven't been challenged to a life of surrender, self-denial, and service.

Chapter 8

Discipleship Redefined

The church lost its way when it became entangled in the expansive web of culture and lifestyle. It has adopted and taught a compromised, incomplete, understated, and therefore misleading and deceptive understanding of discipleship. The result is that the Church is deteriorating, decaying, and dying because we now give a less than inspiring witness that doesn't make a very good impression on our kids or those that we hope to reach with the Gospel.

We in the church blame our decline on the moral decay in our culture, secular humanism, modernism, and science. We portray ourselves as being under siege. We're barking up the wrong tree. This conceptualization of reality and the ways we counter these influences are nothing more than "holy smoke and mirrors." "Smoke and mirrors" is a means of making something appear different than what it is. It is a way of obscuring the truth using misleading information. It refers to a concept that, when examined closely, proves to be an illusion. Here it is being applied to the church to describe our tendency to blame the culture for our decline, rather than looking for the reasons internally. We are responsible for our own demise. Blaming the culture is a deflection that distracts us from looking inward.

A huge factor in the reason for our decline is our almost total and complete failure to give a witness that catches people's attention and causes them to sit up and take notice of whose we are and who we serve. Our attempts to witness fall flat because of our failure to live dedicated and committed lives as disciples. The deceptive explanations we have given for the decline have obscured the truth. Using "holy smoke and mirrors," we have created an alternative reality where we see ourselves as faithful disciples. The alternative reality has become so much a part of who we are that we no longer consider the possibility that we are not only responsible for the decline, but that we have been co-conspirators in the process. We have allowed discipleship to be redefined, and it is astounding that it happened without the church intending to do so or realizing what it had done. The church inadvertently, unknowingly, and unintentionally allowed it to happen.

Now we're here. Discipleship has been redefined and the core of Christianity has been compromised. The biblical portrait of a disciple is a person just like us, seeking the help of the Holy Spirit to be Jesus' servant presence in the world. Some might say, "Just look at all the good the church has done." The truth is, with very few exceptions, the lives of church members do not validate what we say and believe. Very few of us live out our lives as faithful disciples. Very few hear the kind of preaching and teaching that "calls us out" to live as dedicated, faithful disciples. Using "holy smoke and mirrors," the church has redefined discipleship, compromised the Gospel, and lost its soul.

People are searching for meaning. Some are searching for forgiveness, healing, and peace. Some are looking for genuineness and authenticity. Others are looking for comfort, help, and hope, and some are lonely, afraid, and longing for a new start. The Gospel speaks to all of this. The Gospel heals and transforms. When recreated through the obedience, suffering, death and resurrection of Jesus Christ, we are called to a life of obedience, the disciple's life of self-denial and service. It is the latter that is deemphasized, minimized, understated, and emptied of its essence and completeness. The "God really cares about us" part is great, but that's where the message stops. The chain of care is broken. The "really care" part, that refers to making sacrifices so we can serve others, gets short-changed, bigtime.

Our efforts are token at best, and at their worst, they are the responses of Christian narcissists - ungrateful folks who only think of themselves. We hear the Gospel promise of forgiveness and are assured that things are straightened out with God. Then, once again, we let God take a back seat in our lives. We hear people witness that they don't know how they would have made it through without Him. Then, we fail miserably when it comes to showing the same concern for the pain, loneliness, and suffering of others, those who are forgotten, abandoned, marginalized, destitute, and don't know how they are going to make it. God calls us to help them. God calls us to reach out to them with every fiber of our being and to not "grow weary of doing good" (Galatians 6:9).

God notices when discipleship is diluted and then passed off for the real deal. We are giving people the first level of what they are desperately seeking, which is something very different from the whole enchilada of what the Christian life is all about. We receive in abundance, but are not quite so eager to share it to help bind up the wounds and brokenness of so many in the world. The Church has lost its soul.

Being a Christian for a long time doesn't make life any easier either. Even long-time Christians wonder if it's all worth it or if God even notices. However, we have an anchor that is tied to an event. Jesus was stripped and beaten, and gave His life for us on the cross. This makes a difference because we are assured that we are now held in hope. This is the type of reassuring message that we want to hear when we're experiencing strife or failure, or when we are lonely or afraid. We have an anchor that is our hope. His love surrounds us in the eye of the storm. This is what we want to hear. People want to hear that Christ can bring healing wherever there is emptiness, guilt, anxiety, and depression. What we look for in the church is comfort, support, and reassurance.

Then we are called to be disciples, where discipleship is stated in terms of obedience to His commands. Unfortunately, it is an "obedience" which is not fully explained and which we are left to figure out for ourselves. We need to be emphasizing that we are the ones who bring Christ's comfort to others. As disciples, we are the ones who are called to bring to others the assurance of the power of the resurrection that helps us to pick up the broken pieces of our lives.

This explains the lack of conviction and commitment with which the church witnesses to those who don't know Christ and serve those in need. Church is the place to go when we need help with healing, hurt, pain, sadness, and heartache. This is the meaning of church for most Christians. We are looking for spiritual strength, consolation, refuge for the weary, help in time of trouble, someone to walk with us, stand by us, and come to our aid – "No more sorrow, No more pain." We find it in the music, the preaching and teaching, the words of the worship leader, and the prayers. All of this leads to a distorted description of what a disciple looks like. While God may run many subsidiary businesses, this is what we consider to be the original company, the identity of the corporation, the brand that defines the product. What we want from our church is forgiveness, life, salvation, and help and comfort in all our sorrows, troubles, difficulties, and burdens. We also want preaching and teaching about discipleship where obedience to His commands is not spelled out in specifics that call for surrender, commitment, and sacrifice. Guess what? The Christian church, in all of its denominations and expressions, is there to accommodate us. Discipleship has been redefined, the core of Christianity has been compromised, and the church has lost its soul.

Living the Dream

We became entangled in the web of lifestyle and culture, and lost our way because of our compromised, incomplete, understated, and therefore misleading and deceptive understanding of discipleship. We tend to focus on the general passages, while glossing over the powerful passages with the specifics; this model of discipleship is fatally flawed. Concepts like selflessness and self-sacrifice are absent from the mix. We end up leaving a phenomenal amount of untapped potential at the altar. We could be serving many more folks than we do. Again, if we have honestly never stopped to think about all this, that's one thing, but once the issue has been surfaced and brought into our awareness, and we don't make any changes, that is another matter completely. It's called indifference. Using "holy smoke and mirrors," a lot of noise and distraction by pointing to the culture's attempts to attack and weaken the church, we manage to nurture the illusion of significance and relevance, while concealing the truth, namely, that we have redefined discipleship.

We underemphasize the passages that are quite specific. We find a way to interpret and spin the definition of discipleship in a way that helps us repress and deny what the Scriptures explicitly teach. It's not like all of this is buried somewhere in the fine print.

The church became comfortable and content in the growing wealth of the middle class. We adopted ministry plans that were less than visionary and challenging, given the possibilities for significant increases in offerings. We were swept along with the significant increases in the standard of living and the step-up in lifestyle, and lost our way. It just sort of happened, and nobody noticed. It happened because we accommodated ourselves to the good life and the American Dream. We didn't realize we needed to go through some major changes in order to retain our core values. Teaching about discipleship was compromised, and we lost our passion, vitality, and energy.

The church's accommodation to the culture was seamless. Isn't that the way it works with sin? We are just as vulnerable to the materialistic tendencies of our consumer economy as everyone else. During an expanding economy, everyone adapts to the accumulation of more stuff and more wealth; the same is true in the church. We were living the dream. In the midst of rapid growth in wealth accumulation, the job description of a disciple was modified to the point where one would have to say that discipleship has been redefined.

To be sure, the process of redefining discipleship has to be understood within the context of recent history. The industrial revolution transformed Europe between 1750 and 1850. During that time, the fledgling economy of our new nation was starting to grow rapidly. Early on we found it necessary to deal with issue of slavery, which was only resolved by, as Lincoln put it, "a great civil war, testing whether that nation, or any nation so conceived and so dedicated, could long endure." Imagine being a church member at that time. Think about what was on their minds and hearts and in their prayers when they gathered for worship. At the very heart of the conflict was the abolition of slavery and the South's fears about how it would impact their economy. After the war, the nation's economy continued to grow due to the industrial revolution in our cities. Between 1860 and 1920, the United States became the leading industrial and manufacturing power in the world. The foundation that supported the growth of middle class wealth was now in place. Wages and the standard of living were increasing. Then, the church's attention was diverted by two world wars and a depression.

However, advances in the application of the principles of Christian stewardship didn't keep pace with the expanding economy. The population was increasing, churches were growing, and offerings were going up. Lulled into complacency, there didn't seem to be much of a need for it. The clergy were happy as membership and contributions increased. They welcomed the significant increase in offerings to remodel, build additions, raise salaries, and add staff. Capital campaigns were possible without having to challenge folks to the degree where they would get upset. The "smoke and mirrors" of growth and expansion gave the appearance of a healthy church. In the midst of this amazing economic expansion, the clergy didn't challenge members to use their newfound wealth to fund an expansion of mission and ministry that, up to that time, would have been unthinkable.

It was all too easy. On the inside, the church was in the early stages of disease, gradually compromising its core mission and values. There was a lack of passion for lost souls and no urgency to seek out the poor and suffering of the world. Church members were focused on their pursuit of the American Dream, while setting aside precious little time for sacrificial service as volunteers. I think it is fair to say that everybody was happy. Nobody saw the necessity of speaking with a prophetic voice about a life of sacrificial service that flowed from disciples overwhelmed by, and responding to, God's grace. The good times were rolling, and the call to discipleship and sacrificial service was rarely heard.

How did we get led astray? How were we deceived? As the economy began to expand, the standard of living of a growing middle class improved, and a whole lot of folks went along for the ride. The church was not there with the stewardship education needed to help us understand the expanded opportunities presented to us as beneficiaries of the new and growing middle class. We weren't even aware that some of our core values had been compromised. We had been sucked in and didn't realize it was happening. Now it's too late. It's a done deal. There's no turning it around. The Church has lost its soul.

It just happened. As the standard of living continued to rise, the church allowed the meaning of discipleship to change, as it kept accommodating itself to the changes in the culture. The essence of what it means to be a disciple morphed into something that is quite different from the biblical understanding of the term. It just happened, and we missed it.

Well Intentioned

I totally understand who we are, how we became this way, and where we are now. Those of us who have taught a diluted, sanitized, and compromised version of discipleship, that allows wiggle-room, are sincere and genuine. We are well-intentioned, well-meaning servants who made an honest mistake, having tried the best we could with the awareness and understanding we had. We want to follow God and do His will. Our love is genuine. We are dedicated people. The last thing we want to do is to discredit the church, defame the church's character, create stumbling blocks for unbelievers, or lead people astray. We are indeed trying to move the church in a direction that is faithful to its New Testament roots.

The intent in all of this is not to judge, blame, criticize, condemn, or chastise those who haven't lived as disciples, or those whose teaching allows for wiggle room. I empathize with them. I totally understand how this has happened. I get it. We sincerely believed we were following the Lord's will, but we were sincerely and genuinely mistaken. We were caught up in the cultural changes that accompanied the broad development of materialism and consumerism. I get it! I am there too!

We recently received post cards in the mail from two local congregations as part of their outreach to the community. One read:

Connect with God
Connect to a community of believers
Connect with the Bible
Connect with a deeper life
Connect with direction
Connect with meaning
Connect with purpose
Connect with your reason for being

The other read:

Fall is in the air! This season, don't fall into the old back-to-school, back-to-work routine. Celebrate the season by kindling new friendships and igniting your spiritual life! At Legacy (Christian Church), you'll discover warm fellowship for those cool autumn mornings. Enjoy fresh messages that are relevant and inspiring, as well as modern music and a loving, educational children's program. Come join us – we're saving a place for you.

I do appreciate and give thanks for their efforts. Nevertheless, what was conspicuously absent was any mention of the call to a life of self-denial and service in response to all that God has done for us, which is rarely mentioned in the process of bringing people into membership. Is this being picky? It is not intended that way. It is not intended to be judgmental or critical. We all do the same thing in our efforts to try to provide an entry point into a relationship with Christ.

Whether a congregation is the real deal or not depends on what they mean by "deeper life," "direction," "meaning," "purpose," and "inspiring." While I realize discussions about discipleship can begin after people become members, truth be told, rarely do we get to the discipleship part. Sadly, my sense is that we hardly give it more than lip-service, both for newcomers and those who are already members. I've heard pastors talk about their members as if they are "the salt of the earth," "saints on earth," or "beautiful people." This can be misleading. Are they living out the biblical description of what it means to be a disciple? Have they been given the impression that what they are doing is God pleasing, and that they are good Christians? Should we challenge them, or allow them to go on thinking that they can live God pleasing lives by continuing to do what they have been doing?

The overwhelming majority of Christians today have likely never been shown the full and complete picture of what it means to be a disciple. We are left to figure it out for ourselves. There is a timidity in teaching a Christianity that does not compromise the meaning of living lives of obedience and surrender. It is perfectly understandable that, by default, Christians learn a partial, incomplete, compromised version of Christianity and the call to discipleship. Somewhere along the road to Christian maturity, we have to teach a complete and accurate description of what being a disciple is all about.

My experience as a pastor has taught me that, as long as we describe discipleship in broad strokes and general terms, people can discount what Christianity, discipleship, and church membership look like. We don't grasp the fullness of what a walk with the Lord is all about. Immature Christians rationalize and justify the validity of their own compromised version of discipleship. This allows them to avoid making a total commitment to a life of loving service. The vast majority just don't get it when discipleship is explained in terms of Jesus being the center of our lives, the One who gives meaning and purpose to our lives, the One who is our reason for being, and the One who is our everything.

Most do not dedicate themselves to serving the Lord with all their being. A life of joyful, willing, and complete obedience simply does not follow. However, whenever the foreign language of discipleship gets translated into plain English, people get defensive. When we get concrete and specific, folks think we're unrealistic and out of touch. We're not. This is foundational for Christianity. We need to ask how it is that we are to live out the command to "love one another," how to live out what it means to be a disciple in the context of a church that is continuing to decline into insignificance and irrelevance.

Desensitized to Materialism and Consumerism

Judging, blaming, and criticizing pastors because they found themselves caught in these powerful forces is certainly not appropriate. It would be wrong to throw them under the bus. While we in the clergy weren't helpful in providing the spiritual guidance and direction needed to cope with the insidious nature of the spiritual virus that has infected and weakened the whole church, it came out of nowhere. It caught us all off guard. It just happened, and we all enjoyed it. We had been desensitized to the temptations of materialism and consumerism. The church was growing and we were kept busy tending to the spiritual needs of our flocks.

The current understanding of discipleship is now so much a part of who we are as a church that, except for a tiny remnant of the faithful, the die is cast. Those who might try to lead an effort to reclaim who we are by preaching and teaching biblical discipleship, will, at best, be discounted. At worst, they will encounter stiff resistance, strong objections, and outright rebellion. The preacher will be labeled radical, unrealistic, misguided, or impossibly idealistic. It is a tough sell, even for the Holy Spirit.

Biblical teaching about what it means to be a disciple is a huge threat to commonly held views. Core beliefs and core values are called into question, as we are, in effect, being asked to reconsider bedrock convictions about life, purpose, and meaning. It is not easy to step back and respond in a calm, collected, and rational way when part of the very foundation of everything we believe and have been teaching is being questioned. We have to confess to our members that what we have been teaching about discipleship was not accurate and reteach the truth - a truth that is a hard pill for the laity to swallow. The rank and file among the laity would not sit idly by if sacrifice and self-denial became a priority. The almost unanimous consensus about current views of stewardship and discipleship is here to stay.

Am I all wet? Are my views totally off the wall, strange, weird, or misguided? How likely is it that I'm on the right track and that almost the whole church has got it wrong? It sure would be nice if I was wrong.

There is no doubt that our preaching and teaching exacerbates the problem as we consciously choose to allow our members to remain insulated from the full impact of the call to discipleship. We cut our members too much slack, allowing them to be way too comfortable on a journey where they could be so much more faithful and find so much more joy and peace in lives of sacrifice and loving service.

Understandably, we reach a point in our life of sin where we no longer even see sin as sin. John Burns explains it this way, "When someone spends enough time divided from God they get used to the darkness; the soul adjusts to the gloom like the eye to dimmed light. [. . .] Over time, sin mires the heart and chains it to earthly pursuits until it no longer recalls the sweetness of [the] movement toward God."[67] When we do give serious consideration to our own sinfulness, we end up giving ourselves the benefit of the doubt. We say to ourselves, "Well, I'm not that bad. I have my faults, but basically, I'm a good person."

Sadly, we have been misled and pulled into the delusion that we are good Christians. We all have our views about what life is about, who we are, how we got here, and what our purpose is. The philosophies, beliefs, convictions, and perspectives of the people who have raised us and taught us, have shaped our lives. We integrate the various elements of life we have been taught and experienced into our own world view. Each of us has a framework for our perceived reality. We get accustomed to that reality, accommodate ourselves to it, and get comfortable living in it. These principles and convictions become the anchors that give our lives purpose and direction.

Christians get caught up in a delusion that permeates the culture in which we have been nurtured. We have accommodated ourselves to the conceptual framework of our culture. There is no reason to question the cultural view that we are kind, caring, and charitable people. These cultural assumptions help make it easy to explain why we do not question whether or not we have strayed from the biblical understanding of discipleship.

Given the context of our own economic realities and the choices open to us in pursuit of the American Dream, each of us has to ask how our decisions impact others and whether we are really any different than the average person. We measure ourselves by others in our society, rather than by a higher standard of morality, decency and respectability. We have become comfortable with our lifestyle and have lost a sense of indignation about the serious injustices and inequities of our time

In I Corinthians 15:58, Paul says, "Therefore, my beloved brother, be steadfast, immovable, always abounding in the work of the Lord." The NIV says, "Give yourselves fully to the work of the Lord." The church dances around what those words mean. Paul invites us to come and join in the struggle to live out these words, but in his sermon, as in almost 100 percent of the sermons I have heard or Christian books I have read, the specifics of what the struggle with materialism, consumerism, and the "good life" is all about have not been taught clearly enough. It's not clear what we are being invited to struggle with when we don't have the specifics. The church is surely not stirring the pot. We don't want to ruffle anyone's feathers or step on anyone's toes in an effort to emphasize the importance of engaging in the struggle. We accommodate our message to suit the wishes of the congregation. We bail and compromise the truth.

There was a short window of opportunity when we might have been able to turn the ship in a new direction. Not anymore. It happened so slowly that we were desensitized to the cultural description of what it means to be a good person and accommodated ourselves accordingly. At this point, I'm totally cynical and don't hold any hope that the Church will attempt a major course-correction.

Living a Lie

We have to choose between the values of our consumer-driven, materialistic culture, on the one hand, and the life of a self-giving, self-sacrificing, selfless servant, on the other. Kieschnick captures the essence of the point. "We need to be careful that we don't read our own values and ideas into the Bible. [. . .] Many pick and choose the ideas they want to include in their belief system, and dismiss the teachings they don't want to include."[68] We have defined for ourselves what it means to be a disciple. Rather than measure ourselves by the high biblical standard of discipleship that was been established centuries ago, we use a compromised, contaminated version that reflects the views of the consumer-driven, materialistic culture in which we live. We are not the generous, charitable, compassionate people we think we are. While Christians have more reason than anyone to be charitable toward those in need, our lives aren't noticeably different from everyone else.

We seem to feel we have the freedom to disregard what the Scriptures say and pick and choose what we like and don't like and what we will accept and not accept of the preaching we hear. If we don't like what we're hearing from the pulpit, we tune it out. We formulate our own belief system in a way that is consistent with what we want God to be like. The degree of obedience, commitment, and surrender associated with our own belief system usually involves a minimum of inconvenience and sacrifice. When our claim to be Christians is followed by a life that lacks commitment and passion about walking with the Lord, it becomes a stumbling block for our kids and those who we hope to lead to the Lord.

Some people listening to a challenging sermon respond, "He didn't really mean that! Nobody can live that way. We'll just keep our heads down, fly under the radar, and keep doing things the way we want." Many of us have the attitude that we don't have to listen to what the pastor says. We feel we have the right to take it or leave it, the right to live our life any way we want, even if the Bible teaches something different.

Jesus is the Lord of our lives, not just the Savior of our souls. We are called in the Gospel to put Him first in our lives. It just doesn't happen. When we don't, we are left with a watered-down version of what discipleship. We Christians don't get it. We don't realize how far we have strayed from the path of discipleship. Blessed beyond measure, we come up short in living according to His will for our lives. We just want the God who comforts, encourages, forgives our moral lapses, and cleans up our messes.

The Laundered Version of Discipleship: No Sacrifice Needed

We often hear people say, "He was a good person," "He was always ready to help," or "He would do anything for anybody." While sayings like these give comfort to the family and friends of a departed loved one, they cause a great deal of confusion and misunderstanding when applied to disciples. They convey a partial and incomplete standard of sacrifice and service. Those who make statements like these are simply not aware of the culture's influence in emptying "discipleship" of most of its meaning. Why would we even question an element of American religion that most accept as being a given? It's a non-issue. This is just how it is. Everybody knows that.

Materialism has become so much a part of our DNA that we are unable to see that we really don't care all that much about others. Somewhere in this mix, each of us can figure out why we have accommodated ourselves to a compromised version of discipleship. How is it that we find it so hard to admit it and let go of our attachment to stuff? Our lifestyle developed without having to make a conscious choice as to whether to go along with the biblical teaching of discipleship or not. The values of our culture are so much a part of us that we aren't even aware that it has happened. It wasn't planned. It wasn't something we set out to do. Our spiritual leaders didn't get it either. We were totally unaware that the dumbing down of discipleship was happening and had no clue about how we came to be where we are.

Preaching tends to address minor missteps and small slips, and uses only broad, vague, and general allusions to being disciples. It avoids our need to address social issues, especially those related to poverty, exploitation, and injustice. Preaching often focuses on encouragement and hope for those going through difficult challenges, the need to take responsibility for hurting others in relationships, and how much we could do together if we were to give only two percent more. This trend doesn't begin to approach the gravity of our rebellion against God. Without being made aware of the seriousness of our sin, we are assured of forgiveness too quickly and too easily. Most sermons are a soft-sell.

While recognizing that every sin is serious, in that it shows we are not walking with the Lord and are in danger of further distancing ourselves from Him, most sermons do not convey the seriousness of our having strayed so far from God's will and ways that we are hardly recognizable as Christians. Restricting the focus to our relatively minor incursions into sin allows us to continue to maintain the illusion that we are spiritually secure in our walk with the Lord, unaware that we are in a very precarious position. We do not hear that, as Christians, our life is no longer our own, and that we now live for Him and serve Him with all of our being, showing our love for Him by loving our neighbor.

The evangelistic outreach of the church has been compromised by how economics has driven the values of our culture. I no longer pray for another revival or a new awakening. That's a waste of time. An indescribable sadness and depression washes over me as I realize that we, as the church, don't get it. We don't get what it means to be a disciple. We have been duped by the cultural definition of success, the good life, and the American Dream. My prayer is that there will be at least a few Christians who will get what it means to be a disciple, and in so doing, find peace, the peace that passes all understanding.

Be the Rock [Priest] and Rock the Boat [Prophet]

We waffle when we don't preach and teach the biblical description of a disciple. We waffle when it is time to teach the specifics. We waffle when we use levels of sacrifice that understate biblical understanding. We teach a concept of discipleship with which we can live. Discipleship needs to be so much more.

What I was taught at the seminary was to be a spiritual shepherd, preaching and teaching the saving Gospel of Jesus Christ, caring for the sick and aging, and comforting those going through trials and troubles, all of which are vitally important. What I wasn't taught was to speak the prophetic voice of the One calling people to the life of a dedicated disciple. Seminary was, in effect, all about being taught to be the humble servant and shepherd, who is the rock to whom people turn when they are seeking comfort. If we are not careful, this can lead to our becoming enablers of a lifestyle. It took me a long time to figure this out. It took me a long time see it differently and to learn that there was more to it. Gradually, God's Word became clear and my faith grew stronger. At that point, I understood that it was part of my responsibility to rock the boat by relaying God's prophetic call to a life of discipleship. Maybe the seminaries and Bible colleges of other denominations do this already. However, judging by the minimalist understanding of discipleship practiced by all Christians, when it comes to teaching biblical discipleship, my hunch is we all misunderstand it, and we all come up short.

At first, I was surprised that at least one group of Christians couldn't figure this out. It soon became clear, however, that the tugs and pulls of our culture are just so appealing and enticing that none of us can resist. Given the many passages of Scripture that describe what discipleship is like, how did we let this happen? How is it that none of us get it right? Maybe it is because none of us wants to figure it out and get it right. Since an unequivocal proclamation of the Gospel that includes a biblical description of discipleship is really not what Christians want to hear, have we become part of a conspiracy of silence that helps to keep down the cost of discipleship.

As clergy, we waffle when preaching and teaching about discipleship. We use the eloquent rhetoric of inspirational passages without adding the specifics. When we refer to the passages that lack clarity and specificity, we, in effect, give our blessing to church members as they continue to enjoy the dramatic increase in standard of living, without challenging them to higher levels of sacrificial, first-fruits giving and service. We have lost our focus on what the church is all about, namely, forgiveness, sacrifice, and service.

An essential element of repentance is a thorough and complete understanding of the pervasiveness of our sin as not just involving moral failures, but our complete rebellion against God by a refusal to submit to His will. We have gutted the concept of discipleship, and nobody is talking about it. Now, I'm struggling mightily with whether I should say something that might help to bring this issue out in the open. What I can't figure out is why no one else has brought up this issue. What am I missing?

We didn't even realize that we were waffling. We were just as blinded and just as much in the dark as the laity. We didn't realize what was happening either. Our biblical study was sincere. Our meditation, reflection, and prayer were humble and well-intended. We focused on being faithful in preaching and teaching the Gospel, devoted ourselves to providing pastoral care for the flock at times of sadness and celebration, committed ourselves to sharing the Gospel with the unchurched and the de-churched, and, together with the congregation, tried to serve those in need in the community.

Discipleship is no longer understood to be a Christ-like life of total surrender and commitment, a life of self-denial and service.

Casey Kegley, a fourth-year Master of Divinity student (Concordia Seminary, St. Louis) believes that even with a decline in church attendance and other challenges facing the church, "It's a great time to be in the church, and it's an exciting time to be a pastor." Kegley added, "I feel like more and more what's required for us is to live a life so different and compelling that others wonder at it. If we take seriously what Jesus says, we should look like a pretty strange people who produce curiosity and wonder in others."[69]

For Kegley, it will be an extremely rewarding life as a pastor if he follows what the Bible clearly teaches about discipleship.

A disciple is one whose extraordinary sacrifices are plainly evident. No one can deny that they are living out their faith with total commitment. The intent is definitely there. The tragedy is that our lives don't look anything like what Kegley describes. The consequence of not living out the biblical model of discipleship is that it erodes our credibility and weakens our witness.

Casey and I attended the same seminary. I dedicated my life to faithfully serve the Lord within that tradition. I tried to be a good, caring pastor and shepherd at my first congregation. Early on, however, I began to wonder why our church members weren't living more committed and dedicated lives. It took years before the explanation began to come together. The tragic part is that the explanation isn't all that complicated, but I was too caught up in the traditional paradigm to be able to figure it out.

During the early years of my ministry, I still had not heard of "discipling" members. It was not a concept we used in our circles, or if we did, I missed it. Some congregations do it more intentionally than others. Some don't focus that much on sanctification, and their goals tend to be orientated around the support and maintenance of our faith and the institution. In most of our congregations, most of the abundance of members' time, talent, and treasure available to make an enormous impact on the spiritual and material needs of the poor, suffering, and starving in the world, is wasted. The church has not come anywhere near reaching its potential to serve.

The truth is that for most of our members, these are the kinds of sermons that nobody wants to hear, and they get upset if they are challenged in the way I am suggesting. Consequently, clergy tend to back off. We compromise teaching the totality of the call to what it means to be a follower of Christ. We, as pastors, priests, and leaders, pray that hearts will be set on fire for the Lord. This is great, as far as it goes, but it doesn't mean much unless we also teach what a person with a heart on fire for Jesus looks like. Teaching what it means to be a disciple has to be included as an essential element in our congregation's ministry plan.

Usually, the preacher waffles rather than telling it to us straight. Perhaps at some point, like Casey Kegley, they catch a glimpse of what a disciple looks like, but then, we find a way to repress and bury it somewhere in our subconscious.

The preacher sets the vision. It is we in the clergy who have to decide whether we are willing to preach the sermons our people don't like and don't want to hear. However, most of the members of our congregations are content to remain in "maintenance" mode. When the pastor's vision, preaching, teaching, and leadership do challenge the flock to reach for a higher level of discipleship, the congregation usually comes nowhere near realizing their full potential. The preacher is heartbroken. This is when the ministry gets to be tough. The clergy get down in the dumps and discouraged, and they need our prayers and support.

It is a really big deal to let go of the attraction of a materialistic and pleasure-oriented culture. We don't like the sermons that challenge us to pray for the Holy Spirit's help to let go. We get perturbed when someone dares to suggest that we are not anywhere near as compassionate and charitable as we could be, because we have always seen ourselves as caring, kind, loving, and generous. There is no question that this hits a raw nerve.

We preachers tend to give enough wiggle room to allow our members to remain comfortable with their lifestyle. To say our sermons are not the least bit challenging would be a bit of an overstatement, but not much. Most people never have to deal with the impact of a powerfully challenging sermon. We need to preach the law in a way that encourages reflection and self-examination, using a standard that is high enough to lead us to an awareness of how self-seeking, self-centered, and self-serving we are. We have let culture define discipleship for us, instead of letting the Bible define it for us.

When discipleship is not explained as a self-giving, self-sacrificing, selfless life of service to our Lord, its meaning has been compromised and truth has been distorted. We have to be challenged to sell out for Christ with a life of total devotion. We need to be challenged to look deep into our hearts and figure out what it is that we really believe life is all about and how we are going to respond as we are moved by the Holy Spirit. Being exposed as self-centered, self-serving, and greedy, and then assured that our Lord Jesus Christ won't give up on us and continues to forgive us and love us, is transforming and life changing. As the recipients of abundant blessing, we are called to a life of discipleship, sharing the Gospel, and doing all we can to help those in need.

Christians tend to see themselves as good, decent people, who go to church to be assured their sins are forgiven and that they will be going to heaven. Cheap grace is taking all the gifts and blessings God offers without the follow through that validates what we say we believe, in the eyes of the world. After worship, it's back to business as usual. Those who follow this pattern take advantage of God's love and forgiveness. We take Him for granted, use Him, and dishonor Him. We know the drill. We know how to game the system so we end up being forgiven. We play fast and loose with God's grace, and walk a fine line that borders on contempt.

We are hypocrites who give the outward appearance of respectability, yet come far short of the mark in following God's call to live out the biblical model of discipleship. Our response makes it clear that we aren't living the life of obedience to which we are called by the Gospel. Our walk as disciples is tentative, wishy-washy, and lukewarm. Our life only vaguely resembles the life of discipleship described in the Scriptures. Christians have to accept the truth about themselves before any change is possible. The truth is that we see ourselves doing enough of the right things to consider ourselves good Christians.

One Sunday morning, my concern about the lack of passionate discipleship hit me particularly hard. The hymns, the liturgy, and the Scripture readings seemed especially uplifting to me. They were joyful, encouraging, and comforting, touching several of the awesome and inspiring themes in Christian teaching: that Christ is our strong deliverer, that He is the defender of the weak, and comforts those in need, that He will lift us up on wings like eagles, that the wounded are made whole, and that the captives are free and forgiven. If I was hoping for inspiration, comfort, and assurance, it was all there. What doesn't follow is a clear explanation of the other half of the discipleship part. Scriptural reminders about our response are vague and generic.

A joyful and uplifting worship service does not always translate into a passion to have Christ as Lord of our life. I left church flooded with emotion, conflicted, troubled, discouraged, and even depressed. Transcending moments of being fed by the Word of God left me starving and desperately craving something more – more application that would give me specific examples of what a disciple might do. Recently a brother pastor put it well: "It has been some time since I heard a sermon where I was really challenged."

Members get upset if they are challenged by the biblical understanding of discipleship, or challenged to lead a life of self-denial and service. This is not what they want to hear, and this not the kind of church to which people want to belong. The level of commitment they want is a whole lot less than that of a disciple. What they want is a comfortable, watered-down version of Christianity instead of the real deal. They don't want to hear teaching about the full meaning of biblical discipleship.

This is the kind of sermon nobody likes. The response on a good day might be something like, "Lighten up, Preacher!" On a bad day, "What are you, one of those religious fanatics?" "Where do you get off thinking you can tell us how we should live." "I'll find a church where the preacher sees it the way I do." When we start talking about what a disciple looks like, most Christians get real touchy. Do we want to know what a disciple looks like? Well, here it is. These are precisely the conversations about specifics that we seek to avoid.

Holy Smoke and Mirrors

After the church went through the historical process of redefining discipleship, the core of Christianity was compromised. Using "holy smoke and mirrors," the church has redefined discipleship, compromised Christianity, and lost its soul. We have ripped out large chunks of the biblical meaning of discipleship, and we have been extremely selective in choosing what remains.

"Holy smoke and mirrors" is a fitting idiom for the distorted, understated, and therefore misleading or even deceptive explanation of discipleship that we have passed off as truth. The understanding of the role of the church as a place of forgiveness, healing, hope for the troubled, and comfort for the hurting, is deceptive and misleading in that it is partial and incomplete. It makes church membership appear to be something that it is not. It creates an illusion which doesn't square with scriptural truth.

Knowing that proclaiming Gospel imperatives will ruffle people's feathers and turn them off, we use "holy smoke and mirrors" to soften the message. By doing so, we are not coming clean about our true nature. Our hidden self is different than our public persona. The outcome is that we are showing the world a distorted image of Christianity.

The problem is that it's the brand of Christianity that will sell. It's what Christians want to hear. We have now perpetuated the deception for so long that we can't even see how it has messed us up. So, now it's time to go back and review, searching for a remnant of the now hidden truth. I see some hints of the church's true identity, but where is the rest of it? Through the use of "holy smoke and mirrors," it is well hidden.

The smoke screens put up by destroyers in WWII were meant to conceal the operations of the fleet, so the enemy couldn't see where the ships were or how they were being deployed. Smoke screens provide cover for what is really going on, and mirrors, carefully positioned mirrors, present us with a distorted image that is nothing like the reality they reflect. Using lots of "holy smoke" and strategically placed "mirrors" we have created an altered reality. We have developed a compromised definition of discipleship.

An acquaintance asked what my book was about. I gave him the title and explained it like this, "We, in the church, use holy smoke and mirrors to make it appear we're something we're not; the description of a disciple has been diluted and distorted so much that we, in the church, don't look all that different from everyone else. There is nothing unique or special about us as servants. It has reached a point where we, as the church, have become marginalized, insignificant, irrelevant, and almost useless." His response was immediate, "You're not looking to make any friends, are you?"

Since the church used "holy smoke and mirrors" to develop a compromised, incomplete, understated, and therefore misleading teaching about what it means to be a disciple, how well can we carry out our mission? We're handicapped from the get-go. How can we give an effective witness? Teaching a concept of discipleship that is partial and incomplete explains why the church's witness does not influence people.

The use of "holy smoke and mirrors" resulted in the biggest sell-out in the history of the modern church; in many ways, this development is almost fatal. The church compromised and redefined discipleship so its message would be appealing and acceptable to contemporary Christians. Members are in possession of so much more wealth and free time than anyone could have ever imagined before the twentieth century. Masquerading as disciples, the church has lost its soul and isn't even aware of it. Using "holy smoke and mirrors," repression and denial, blocking and evading, and spin and deflection, discipleship, as practiced, is no longer the concept taught in Scripture. By not clearly teaching what a disciple is, and not living it, the strength of the church has been compromised.

We Live Only for the World

When we preach the sermons most folks don't like to hear, the few disciples who are growing welcome the message and don't get offended. They understand! They get it! They know what we are trying to do. They welcome the reminders because they are constantly fighting the battle to stay focused and to resist the pull of our consumer culture. Those who are Christians know they have to ask for the help of the Holy Spirit every day in order to have any chance of resisting the temptation to live the lifestyle to which our culture says we are entitled.

The reality of the church being a sacrificial servant is a distant memory. What is surprising is that many of those outside the church are even more deeply saddened by what they see than we are. They want us to be so much more. They need us to be so much more, and we let them down.

We aren't ready to sell out for the Lord. Called by the Lord to follow Him? Yes. However, called by the Lord to do it in a manner consistent with the passages teaching selflessness, commitment and sacrifice is not what we signed up for. We draw the line when the call to discipleship gets intrusive and inconvenient and becomes a threat to our goals, hopes, and dreams.

Prophetic preaching that seeks to uncover the truth and expose us for who we are, is not appreciated. Hearers become uncomfortable, angry, and find ways to rationalize and justify lives that are not lived according to God's will. They have their own preferences for the kind of religion they want, picking and choosing Scriptural teachings that are then blended into their own personal brand of Christianity. The appeal of the lifestyle to which they are accustomed effectively sabotages the call to commitment and surrender. In these circumstances, the call to discipleship is difficult to hear and is not popular. When it comes to being disciples, we are frauds, imposters, and pretenders.

Our brand of discipleship is not the real deal. What we practice is counterfeit, and we consequently experience a counterfeit peace. Life is so much less meaningful and satisfying than it could be. We are so much less of a blessing to others than we could be, and, therefore, the church is little more than a shadow of its former self. It is barely recognizable as the community that was called out by Jesus to follow and serve. The church has lost its soul, the very essence of that which makes it what it is. The church has lost its soul and likely won't be getting it back.

The expectations of the flock are accommodated, while the specifics that nail us are avoided. We line up in the pews to get our little spiritual spanking for saying a few bad words or having a few sinful thoughts, while the teaching of what it means to be a disciple is avoided. The bar for being a Christians is not set nearly high enough. When the specifics are omitted, we are implicitly given permission to practice a bland Christianity that lacks commitment, boldness, and fire.

The Bible teaches that believers find favor in the eyes of God only because of the free gift of the forgiveness of sins, offered through Christ's suffering and death on the cross, as our substitute. Then, where there is forgiveness there is also the assurance of eternal life in heaven. However, the rest of the story gets short-changed, namely, how the overwhelming joy and gratitude for forgiveness and eternal life overflows and transforms us into people who express our love and gratitude by living lives totally dedicated to His service, lives that honor our Savior. This last part has been minimized and understated.

In general, people think they are making a good faith effort to live by the Golden Rule: "Do unto others as you would have them do unto you." Frankly, I'm surprised we admit that we even know the Golden Rule. Unless I am mistaken, we sure don't live by it. We either don't understand it or don't want to. Nevertheless, somehow we have convinced ourselves that we do. We believe that we have at least made an acceptable effort to live according to it. While we see ourselves as caring, kind, loving, and generous, the truth is that we are spiritually bankrupt. Our lives are nothing like the members of the orders of the middle-ages and Renaissance with their vows of poverty, chastity, and obedience, which validated what they said they believed and gave them credibility.

In our teaching of discipleship, we don't make clear, definitive statements. Using examples, we need to explain what being a disciple looks like. We need to be a lot more precise and specific. The specificity has to be increased a hundredfold. Otherwise, we will find a way to avoid the really tough part, a life of self-denial and sacrifice. We have hood-winked, snookered, and bamboozled our people into adopting a model for faith-life that is not the real deal. It's almost like we have been hypnotized and are now living a reality that we have created for ourselves, rather than the biblical reality of discipleship. We are living out a delusion. Then, we support and reinforce each other's beliefs and behaviors that are consistent with our corporate delusion.

Even though there are some differences in biblical teaching among denominations and expressions of Christianity, the striking commonality is that we share a fatal flaw. We all teach a partial, incomplete, diluted, and compromised understanding of discipleship. In so doing, we have created our own religion, a religion that does not call for surrender and sacrifice. We think "we can negotiate the terms and conditions of our relationship with God."[70] Simply put, it's what happens when "the church exchanges God-given grace for human religiosity."[71] The temptation of having at least a part of the American Dream within reach influences us to put our affections on this life. "His (Luther's) ire was also meted out upon the Wittenbergers [. . .], since he said they had had the Gospel, but seemed to live only for the world."[72] I totally understand how we have come to where we are. Once discipleship was redefined, a part of the essence of Christianity was compromised and the church lost its soul.

Chapter 9

On Its Last Legs

We now live the redefined model of discipleship that results in a less than inspiring witness. Others don't see much of a difference, if any, between the way they live their lives and the way we live ours. Those who are not Christians do not see the differences they would expect to see in our lives, based on what we claim to believe about a loving, accepting, self-sacrificing God who died on the cross in our place, that we might have forgiveness and eternal life. They do not see us as humble, forgiving servants who seek to meet need wherever we find it. The Christ-like life, so beautiful to behold, is rarely found.

They "hear" the sermons we preach through what they see in our lives, note the obvious inconsistencies with what we preach and teach, and are turned off. They look at how we live and they are not impressed. Sadly, they see us as just as self-seeking, self-centered, and self-serving as others. Our witness is so damaging. They don't want anything to do with Christianity. The outcome is that the church is deteriorating, decaying, and dying.

We are our own worst enemy. We are proceeding in a manner that is counterproductive. We undermine our efforts to carry out our mission and the reason we exist, spreading the Gospel of Jesus Christ. The world listens to us, looks at us, and finds it isn't able to respect what it is that we believe and stand for.

The church isn't merely tolerating mediocrity by teaching a compromised brand of discipleship, which would, in and of itself, be horrendous. What we are doing is actually worse. We are fostering mediocrity. The way we teach discipleship shapes how we live as disciples. What we leave unsaid and undone has presented the culture an image of mediocrity that will be impossible to shake. Those on the outside of the church read us like a book, and what they see isn't pretty.

We, as the church, are an enigma. We "play" church. If we are close to a preacher and listen carefully, many of them are telling us they can't wait until retirement. They are just putting in their time. It's not like they are playing church the way kids do, imagining a day when they will be a missionary, teacher, or pastor. The kids who "play church" are excited. Many of the adults who "play church" are the ones who are just going through the motions. Rather than committing themselves to prayer, reflection, a thoroughly honest evaluation, and considering what they might do differently, they keep walking along in the same rut, unintentionally dragging their parishioners down with them. Now, we're all stuck in the mud.

The Lord knows that we are just playing church. He knows that we are just going through the motions. This community, that was once a noble, inspiring, compassionate, healing, servant community, is nothing like the spiritually vibrant community that it once was. It is dying. It is on its last legs. It's a joy to be with young preachers who haven't yet lost that fire. It's sad to be with preachers once they come face to face with painful reality.

The world will treat us the way it does the feeble and the aging. We see them sitting in a wheelchair at a nursing home. We may say a few words to them and then move on, taking with us another chunk of whatever dignity they have left. They aren't important and we don't have time for them. Even worse, they sense it when we consider them to be a nuisance. Those elderly people are the church. The way we relate to them is the way the world relates to us. Now, it's to the point where the world doesn't even try to hide what it feels about the church.

If only the world could see us as extraordinarily dedicated people, committed to serving those in need. If only they would look at us with respect, awe, wonder, or amazement. They may see a Mother Teresa, Desmund Tutu, Billy Graham, or Pope Francis. They may see folks we know: a long-time volunteer at the food pantry or rescue mission, a lay minister, a Stephen Minister, a youth pastor, a parochial school teacher, or a faithful pastor, but they don't see enough of us living like disciples. Doctors Without Borders, The Red Cross, and Habitat for Humanity are respected, while the church is often seen as narrow-minded, intolerant, and self-righteous. People conclude that there isn't anything special about the church that would inspire them to want to be a part of it. The church isn't declining because of all of the extreme moral deterioration of the fabric of our culture. The deeper underlying reason is that our witness doesn't inspire those we are trying to reach with the Gospel. Rather, it turns them off.

If we are not totally committed to serve, and, therefore, distinctly different from the world, they won't notice or take a second look at who we are and why we are so different. Therefore, we give no opportunity for the Holy Spirit to gain a hearing and have a chance to do its work - to do its thing. We become a rock that will make men stumble and fall.

Do we do some good? Depends on what we mean by some. Yes, the service provided by Christians throughout the world is important and meaningful. Just ask those who have been served and helped. However, compared to our potential, what we are doing is no more than a drop in the bucket.

Are You Out of Your Mind?

"If we are out of our mind, it is for the sake of God" (II Corinthians 5:13, NIV). Just a few years earlier, Jesus' unbelieving relatives exclaimed, as they observed Him working such long hours that He couldn't find time to eat, "He is out of his mind" (Mark 3:21). People observing us as Christians don't say that about us. They don't see us as passionate, committed, and out of our minds. Why should anyone be interested in what we have to say? Our ethics and morals may be a little better. We may not swear as much, tell as many off color jokes, or live together before marriage, but we still don't look all that different from others in our culture.

The biblical teaching of what it means to be a disciple has become so weakened and understated that it has lost its vibrancy, its power, and its appeal. People, in all religions, have rites and rituals, make offerings and practice almsgiving, charity, and service. There isn't much different or special about us. If we're honest, we'll admit that the vast majority of us practice our Christian religion in a manner that isn't all that different from any other religion. Sadly, there isn't more than a faint hint that we are out of our minds. We have crafted our own belief system with levels of sacrifice that we can handle.

What the church teaches about itself and its mission is distorted, one-sided, and out of balance. Much of what we are drawn to is a Jesus who is the "answer" to all of our burdens, our troubles, our brokenness, our despair, and our hopelessness. The worship leader or pastor will say, "I don't know what's going on in your life, what challenges you're facing, but we pray that you will grow closer to the Lord and find relief and peace."

Our denomination is making a concerted effort to help us improve our sermons, but if these improved sermons are preached from the pulpit of an irrelevant church, who is going to be there to hear them. One morning at breakfast I was in conversation with an acquaintance who didn't even realize that the next day would be the 500th anniversary of the Reformation. He hadn't read about it in the newspaper or heard about it on TV. We had at least five major festival services and celebrations here in the Milwaukee area, and yet he hadn't heard anything about our celebration of the Reformation. This is a guy who is not a religious illiterate. As a salesman, he called on the Amish in Nebraska and knew about the Hutterites and Mennonites. I don't know all of his story yet, but what I do know is that if others are like him, all of our improved sermons will be preached to current members from the pulpits of an irrelevant church that will have little impact in reaching the lost. Within the context of an irrelevant church and the way its members live, act, care, and love, who is going to be interested enough in the church to come and hear our improved sermons?

We have failed miserably to come anywhere near realizing our potential as a spiritual powerhouse. The witness we give lacks the credibility and validation that could have been given by an outpouring of love for the Lord through untiring, compassionate service. We had a chance to be something special; that time has passed. We will never get it back.

It is a joy to see how many of the clergy are trying to address all of this by studying the Bible, reading, meditating, going to conferences, learning about different models for parish renewal, and studying revitalization. In our circles, some attend the Parish Leadership Institute, Passionate Believers conferences, or the Change or Die Conference to learn strategies that have worked elsewhere. We attend conferences designed to help us improve our sermons. However, we simply have to recognize that we're doing all of this in the context of an irrelevant church. All of these well-intentioned efforts are undermined and rendered minimally effective because they are based on a false premise, the teaching of a compromised version of discipleship. Given the way we live and act, is anyone going to be interested in the church anyway? Only a few are going to respond to our use of situational evangelism with more than polite courtesy? Only a few are going to be interested enough to want to come and hear our sermons, and what we have to teach? What have we forgotten? We have forgotten that witness needs to be validated by lives that show we really do "love one another."

God's plan is for us to be His presence and do good works, sacrificially serving those who are in need or hurting, and in doing so give witness to Him. John 13:34, 35 says, "A new commandment I give to you, that you love one another: just as I have loved you, you are to love one another. By this all people will know that you are my disciples, if you have love for one another." I Peter 2:12 reads, "Live such good lives among the pagans that, though they accuse you of doing wrong, they may see your good deeds and glorify God." The believer's good life can influence unbelievers to come to Christ.

When we are not challenged to a life of commitment, dedication, and faithful service, the characteristics of a mature faith, and we are not living that way, the world notices. They notice when we relate to others in ways that lack compassion, caring, understanding, reasonableness, thoughtfulness, consideration, and respect. They observe and are not impressed. It is not hard to figure out why the world sees us as self-righteous, judgmental, critical, and intolerant, rather than humble servants meeting needs wherever they are found. They don't see us practicing what we preach. The massive failure of the whole church, to reach its potential for outreach and mission, has resulted in a rapid decline in the reputation and credibility of the church and a resulting decline in membership.

The church has deteriorated and decayed into a community which no longer resembles the communities of the early followers of Christ. It began with the 12 who left all they had to follow Jesus, and who, in the end, remained faithful even though the path for 11 of them led to martyrdom. Over time, the church has degenerated from that lofty total commitment to a lesser, tragically compromised brand of Christianity. Like God's covenant people in the Old Testament, we, as the New Testament people of God, have broken our promises and strayed far from our calling of being a light to the nations.

The church has already lost its soul, and we're not going to be getting it back. We are on our last legs. There can be no ambiguity about this. Any hint of that possibility has to be erased from our minds. Nevertheless, even though there will not be many who will walk with us as disciples, we can be faithful as individuals.

Chapter 10

The Extraordinary Challenge for Today's Disciple

And as he was setting out on his journey, a man ran up and knelt before him and asked him, "Good Teacher, what must I do to inherit eternal life?" And Jesus said to him, "Why do you call me good? No one is good except God alone. You know the commandments: Do not murder, Do not commit adultery, Do not steal, Do not bear false witness, Do not defraud, Honor you father and mother." And he said to him, "Teacher, all these I have kept from my youth." And Jesus, looking at him, loved him, and said to him, "You lack one thing: go, sell all that you have and give to the poor, and you will have treasure in heaven; and come, follow me." Disheartened by the saying, he went away sorrowful, for he had great possessions. And Jesus looked around and said to his disciples, "How difficult it will be for those who have wealth to enter the kingdom of God" (Mark 10:17-23).

I mean, what do we do with this? How can we avoid dealing with it?

How do we respond to the Bible passages that clearly alert us to the danger of getting attached to "stuff," the "good life," entertainment, recreation, and relaxation, which can easily drain our resources and crowd-out time for service? Do we pick and choose the beliefs that we want to be part of our religion? Equipped with the biblical description of a disciple, it's time to examine ourselves to see how we measure up and whether, with the help of the Holy Spirit, we are committed to change. The Scripture's call to discipleship is all-inclusive in its invitation to a life of complete surrender. It is a major hurdle on the road to Christian maturity. The call to discipleship is not just a speed-bump on the road of life; it is more like the obstacles on an advanced course of American Ninja Warrior.

A "Come to Jesus" Moment

We are still a work in progress. As we reflect on the specifics and realize just how far we fall short of living out God's plan for our lives, we come face to face with the truth about ourselves. We know we were sidetracked by an affluent, materialistic, consumer-driven culture, and are overwhelmed by God's mercy and readiness to forgive. With the help and strength of the Holy Spirit, we are ready to renew the pursuit of faithfulness. The call of God in the Scriptures is a call to willing obedience, not something we have to do and not a life where we comply out of fear that there will be hell to pay if we don't. We have been forgiven by the saving work of Jesus Christ. Having received this fantastic, free and undeserved gift, ours' is an obedience that is humbly submissive; it is something we want to do.

Everybody has a story. It is so important for us to listen to each other tell our stories. We will if given a chance. It is often a humbling, enlightening, and sacred journey into the very depths of our being. We all try to figure out what life is about. We are all very important and special to the heavenly Father who loves us so much that He sent His Son to die on the cross for our sins and rise from the grave to guarantee our eternal life in heaven. Yet, until our death, we continue to live on this side of eternity. So our story here on earth is not over.

The blinders I have been wearing have resulted in a long and drawn out process of coming to where I am now. We move from one level of awareness to another, not able to reach the next level without having gone through the one that preceded it. Just a few years ago I tried my hand at expressing where I was in writing. It didn't sell very well, but it was me – it was part of my story. Now at 76, I am amazed at how wonderful it is to continue to be blessed with a spiritual journey that is exhilarating. Wow! What I am praying for is the strength to try to move past the barriers that would lead to a tragic and unfulfilling sidetrack in my life.

What a tragedy it is when people work all their life so they can enjoy their retirement and then discover that what they have waited all their life to be able to do is not all that meaningful and fulfilling. It is such a huge disappointment, one that requires us to take stock of our life, and to reflect and think through how we will choose to live-out the rest of our lives. It is exhilarating when we realize we still have the time, opportunity, and physical strength to be able to commit ourselves to a meaningful and rewarding path of sacrificial service. There are so many lost souls. There is so much pain, suffering, and misery out there.

There is a huge difference between the good church people we think we are and what we're really like. We have more passion about leisure activities, our favorite sports teams, and political discourse than our commitment to a life of loving service – to a life of discipleship. We have this uncanny ability to repress, deny, rationalize, and justify the perception we have of ourselves, which makes it possible to paint a rosy picture. The truth lies buried beneath layers of deception and delusion, where we insulate and protect ourselves from the painful truth. The question is, are we willing to re-examine our current level of commitment, and, asking for the guidance and strength of the Holy Spirit, try to change our lifestyle, reorder our priorities, and make sacrifices in order to do much more to help others. We have so much potential to be able to help the neediest and most vulnerable among us.

Hearing a frank, honest, and unvarnished description of discipleship really makes us uncomfortable. It irritates, agitates, and gets under our skin in a way that crosses the line into the dreaded realm of the "religious fanatic." If that is our reaction, we still haven't been crushed by the weight of our sin – what we are really like. We have yet to have our "come to Jesus moment."

We've had our chances to do something about human need, pain, suffering, and misery. We've dropped the ball. To the degree that this is an issue for each of us, we contribute to evil and suffering through sins of omission. There is an inner conflict as we go about the process of deciding how much we will contribute and how much time we spend as volunteers. We have to address our personal struggle with what it means to live as a disciple. We try to avoid the tension and push it out of our awareness as much as possible. Each of us has to come to terms with the meaning of life.

The LSD Hallucination: Less Sacrificial Discipleship

So where does that leave us? What's next? Each of us has to evaluate the level of our charitable giving and volunteer service. Accomplishing that task requires that we become aware of the standard by which we measure. Are we flowing along with the current of culturally accepted norms and part of the conspiracy of the ordinary? Do we seek to benefit from the collusion that maintains low expectations, or do we want to consider another norm for service and sacrifice? We need to make a conscious choice about the standard by which we will measure ourselves.

Do we choose the path of hard work in pursuit of getting more stuff and our share of the American Dream, or do we work hard so that we can provide for the basic needs of our families, and as many of the unmet needs of others as we can? Are we ready to make a commitment to the practice of charitable giving and volunteer service that seeks to do everything possible to address the unmet needs of others?

The sermons I've heard about being transformed into people who are more caring and compassionate servants convey a beautiful vision. However, the vision is flawed because we fall into the trap of measuring ourselves by culturally accepted norms. There are other norms. One in particular is rooted in Christ. Mother Teresa's norm was the sacrificial, self-giving, selfless life of Jesus, which we can use to determine whether we are truly caring, compassionate servants, and by which we can evaluate our charitable giving and volunteer service. She concluded that she didn't measure up to the standard by which she measured herself—God's standard as taught in His Word. We have to go through that same process. We have to be clear about the standard by which we evaluate ourselves and then determine whether we "measure up" and whether we think we are loving, decent, and morally upright, or not. How much are we helping and giving when compared to our potential? We are all too willing to whitewash the truth.

There are certainly many "wow" people who have been transformed by the Gospel, and who offer themselves completely in sacrificial service to our Lord. They give their all as dedicated disciples and would agree with my thesis. These folks are humbly submissive. They rejoice in and are thankful for all that Christ has done for them, and they seek the strength of the Holy Spirit so they can continue to serve Him faithfully.

It is those who resist the call and invitation to walk more faithfully as servants who are likely to get upset, or even angry. They are the ones who are offended and become defensive or even irate, when anyone dares suggest that they are not anywhere near as compassionate and generous as they could be. These people are experiencing an LSD hallucination, that is, having the spiritual experience of an escape from the reality that they are living a life of less sacrificial discipleship. They experience an altered state of thoughts, feelings, and awareness, accompanied by frequent flashbacks, a perception disorder that helps maintain the delusion that we're good church people, rather than what we're really like.

For those who "get it," it is not just a rude awakening, but a devastating experience of shame and guilt. After it sinks in, we are humbly and gratefully reminded again of the incomprehensible love of a God who knows exactly how we have lived and still forgives us. We have been richly blessed and have the potential to do great things in the realm of volunteer service and charitable giving.

Many do give to church and charity. As noted, my sense is that we give enough to salve our consciences, but nowhere near our potential. We have become comfortable with a bar that has been set way too low. We have distorted concepts like caring, kindness, compassion, service, and generosity to the point where they have lost much of their meaning and what stirs the deepest of emotion and passion. Those who have a deep and abiding concern for the needs of all humanity and a willingness to make a sacrificial commitment to do everything possible to alleviate human need and suffering are few.

Tom Brokaw said, "I'm paid very well for what I do. I have enough money to keep myself comfortable. [. . .] My kids are working [. . .] [and] have the thrift gene passed down from their grandparents. At the same time, if their needs get critical, they've got dad around to help out."[73] Obviously, we don't all have parents who are in a position to be able to do the same. As Christians, we are the brothers and sisters of those who don't. We need to monitor how much of our time and treasure we contribute to church and charity, evaluating our circumstances, and settings goals. Giving 5, 10, 25, 40 or 60 percent of available resources does not determine whether we are generous. It's how much we give of what we have that is beyond what we really need that determines whether or not we are generous. The value to the recipients does not change and is very important to them, but if we are not as generous as we could be, others in need go unserved.

In America, almost all of us are wealthy, richly blessed people who have the means and opportunity to live self-giving and selfless lives of sacrifice and loving service. By the world's standards, we are wealthy people. We have food, clothes, a roof over our heads, a car, cell phones, a large flat-screen TV, a computer, an iPad, and enough for a meal out once in a while. Most of us can save enough for a little vacation. Yet, we take so much for granted. We may contribute and volunteer regularly, and, touched by the story of a stranger's misfortune, be moved to make a contribution. Nevertheless, we need to be honest with ourselves and search the depths of our being to see if we qualify as people who have compassionate, generous, servant hearts. Can the starving and suffering count on us to meet needs related to nutrition, clean water, basic health care, shelter, sanitation and education?

We live the good life and have the world by the tail. Consequently, the national household average of two percent giving to charity seems like such a pittance. We just don't care all that much about those in need. Within the framework of sins of omission, the failure to contribute generously, becomes a contribution to suffering.

These are hard words for believers to hear. We're not excited about those parts of the Bible where it describes what an obedient response to the Gospel looks like, because they ask for inconvenience and cramp our style. We respond to the unmet needs of others with callous indifference and ingratitude. We just want to be left alone so we can provide for our family, live a respectable life, and enjoy a little of the good life. We get into a comfort zone and don't want anybody to disturb it. If anyone threatens to burst the bubble of reality we have created for ourselves, we get pretty upset. We fiercely resist that which challenges and threatens our world-view and lifestyle. We have been snookered, rationalize and justify our worldview and lifestyle, and, insulate ourselves from all of the pain, misery, and suffering that is out there.

Nevertheless, we plead for forgiveness, and in being forgiven, find the power to persevere. Dietrich Bonhoeffer writes about the call from God to walk with the Lord and our struggles in doing so.

Only the man who follows the command of Jesus single-mindedly, and unresistingly lets his yoke rest upon him, finds his burden easy, and under its gentle pressure receives the power to persevere in the right way. The command of Jesus is hard, unutterably hard, for those who try to resist it. But for those who would willingly submit, the yoke is easy and the burden is light. [. . .] Jesus asks nothing of us without giving us the strength to perform it.[74]

Instead, we try to find a way to combine our affection for this world with our loyalty to Christ. This is tough when an accurate measure of charity and generosity is measured not by the amount given, but by the amount given relative to our net worth. The truth is we all struggle with our human nature when we near the threshold of the emotional pain experienced when we don't want to give any more, even though we know we can.

Every once in a while, we are reminded of biblical teaching and the really compelling "wow" passages describing discipleship that come up in the Sunday Scripture readings, in Bible class, or when reading the Bible at home. We catch a glimpse of it, but it quickly fades away. We begin to get it, and see what we are asked to do, but since it isn't a major emphasis in the church, we are able to deflect those notions before they grab hold of us. Since no one else is paying attention to it, we don't either. We have some idea of what discipleship is about, but since everyone else avoids dealing with it, we do too.

We want our kids to have the clothes and smart phones that most kids have, and we work long hours so we are able to buy, upgrade, or remodel our home. At the same time, others are born in communities and countries where life is very different from what we are used to. On occasion, we hear about the poor and suffering of the world. Then, once again, we get caught up in the pursuit of the American Dream and quickly forget.

In our core, we are self-centered, self-serving, self-seeking, indifferent, insensitive pursuers of the good life. We all have our ways of rationalizing and justifying how much we contribute and the amount of time we serve as volunteers. Our greed is often thinly disguised by token contributions to church and charity and minimal contributions to needs resulting from natural disasters and human tragedy. In truth, we don't give sacrificially or volunteer all that much.

I'm not at all optimistic that things are going to change and that the whole church will become more compassionate; that's simply wishful thinking. For most of us, the response will be minimal. Nevertheless, I hope it would be a wake-up call for the few who will be blessed to discover and celebrate the fullness of joy and peace that accompany the life of sacrifice and service, and that follows the assurances of grace and forgiveness.

Since any changes we make impact our families, we will want to talk with them about how they view the needs of others and where we are going to reach out and care for those in need. Are we going to do it by volunteer service and by contributing to church and charity? If the family doesn't buy in, we have to proceed carefully before making any unilateral decisions about how to allocate all the family's resources. We usually don't have conversations like these and end up doing far less than we could. By omission, we contribute to the pain and suffering of many other families.

We have to be honest. Most of us enjoy a lifestyle of excess. Most Americans who live on "Main Street" have more than enough to be comfortable and enjoy life. We enjoy a comfortable life while millions are starving. We don't seem to care very much about those in great need, struggling just to retain some semblance of human dignity.

Once the soul-searching begins with the urging of the Holy Spirit, a Christian who thinks he is living a good enough life to get to heaven but has never heard the full teaching about discipleship before may recognize the overwhelming need for prayer and repentance. We create an alternate reality for what the world is like. I want so very much to be able to be more hopeful. However, in our consumer-driven economy where it is so easy to get distracted, it just doesn't seem like there will ever be much of a change.

This is how the world works. It always has, and it always will. Everybody does their thing trying try to work out the best deal for themselves. It is the nature of man to operate out of a self-interest that is self-centered, self-serving, and self-seeking. When hearing this message, many of us will respond, "What a depressing message. I'm not going back to that church. I went home feeling worse than when I came." Nevertheless, we must speak this truth, albeit with an understanding, gentle, and caring manner, and with the prayer that the Holy Spirt will work through it to change hearts. I want to believe we can be different, but I just can't. As for our better angels, they simply aren't all that good. We fail to see just how much misery could be alleviated and how much suffering could be relieved, if only we were more concerned about the unmet needs of others.

One would assume that Christians would be different. However, even those of us who are so blessed that our kids have food, shelter, and all of their other basic needs met, do not seem to be deeply troubled, disturbed, moved, or touched by the agony of parents who can't even provide the basics for their children and who sometimes have to watch them die from hunger or disease. It certainly seems as if we are indifferent and don't really care. Insulated from their pain, we are so emotionally detached that we can just go on with our lives without doing anything about their plight. How can we claim to not be hard-hearted, uncaring, and merciless? So many among us who garden, quilt, sew, read, and do ceramics or woodwork, see ourselves as basically good people, and yet remain oblivious to the world of pain and suffering beyond our sitting room, yard, or workshop. We lift little more than a finger to try and do something about others who are in desperate straits. It is one thing to be a decent person, a law abiding citizen, an upstanding member of the community, and a good neighbor, and something totally and completely different to be a caring, compassionate servant of those in need, a citizen of the "holy nation" (I Peter 2:9) that is the family of faith.

These images clash when we reach the threshold at which our basic instincts are triggered, when we feel we are being unfairly asked to sacrifice our standard of living for their well-being. My sense, however, is that for a huge majority the experience of sacrificial charitable giving is more like getting a root canal than a joyful experience reflecting thankfulness for having been blessed by the Lord. Rarely do we demonstrate concern for the needs of others that involves inconvenience or a disruption of our plans and dreams. Rarely do we make commitments that require a significant investment of time or economic sacrifice.

We have this image of ourselves as kind, decent, good people, who, while sinners, aren't all that bad. We don't have the foggiest notion that we are evil, hard-hearted, and merciless. We are clueless! As long as we hang on to an image of ourselves as people of faith, who are walking with the Lord, we all continue to live in alternate reality that serves to conceal a massive deception.

As a consequence, who suffers? Who gets hurt? Not us. We are forgiven. Those in need are the ones who continue to suffer and will continue to suffer until we become aware of how far we miss the mark in terms of being loving, caring Christian servants. Bonhoeffer is spot on in what God thinks about all this. "God will not be separated from our brother: he wants no honor for himself so long as our brother is dishonored."[75]   Admitting that we all mess up once in a while totally understates the point. We are constantly seeking to accumulate far more than what the Bible teaches we need: "But if we have food and clothing (basic needs), we will be content with that" (I Timothy 6:8). This blatant disregard for biblical teaching about good works and discipleship results in our taking a giant step down the path toward creating a belief system that suits our idea of what we want our religion to be like, and allows us to justify the pursuit of our own goals, hopes, and dreams rather than God's.

There Has to Be More Than This

Many wonder what life is all about. On some level, we are all aware that the purpose of life is about more than popularity, accumulating stuff, power, fame, entertainment, recreation, or vacations. We realize that something is missing and that there has to be something more. Some today use the phrase "a life well-lived." What exactly is a life well lived? What is it that brings enough meaning that it gives us a measure of peace? We already know, but really don't want to hear it. We don't want to hear it because what the Scriptures teach about discipleship goes too far for us. It's too radical, too unrealistic, and we don't want the church to get carried away in its teaching. We don't want the church to go off the deep end.

We want to live with enough meaning to be able to tell our children about it – about how much we've accomplished and achieved. However, do we also want to tell them that there are others as important as they are, and that we gave away their inheritance so others would have an opportunity to survive and succeed – the same opportunity we gave them? Do we want to tell them that the playing field is not level, that life is not fair, and that we want to help the suffering, the starving, the poor, and the abandoned, and address the inequities experienced by the disadvantaged and the marginalized? Are we looking for meaning and purpose? This is it! Our personal struggle is with how to respond to what it means to live as a disciple.

The other option is to do enough to give the appearance of being a good Christian, or at least enough to give the appearance of our being good people, enough to quiet our consciences, enough to keep our feelings of guilt in check, enough to suppress the truth through some sort of spiritual amnesia, enough to justify our qualifying as having more than met the minimum standard. Truth be told, we don't want to hear the biblical description of a disciple. Truth be told, we really don't want to get it. All we want is to be able to maintain a façade sustained by deflection and repression, and rationalize and justify our status as members of the church, and sons and daughters of the King. This is the essence of the struggle.

What is it that we really want? We want help in our troubles, trials, and tribulations. We want peace in the midst of turmoil and anxiety. When heartbroken and consumed by grief, we want Jesus to comfort, strengthen, and heal. We want Jesus to uphold us, sustain us, and give us hope. We want Jesus to lift us up when we cry out of the depths of despair. The amazing thing is He does.

However, when life settles down and starts to get back to normal, we return to old patterns. We return to a life where we do not thank, praise, and serve Him with all of our hearts. We turn to Him when we need Him and fall away when we don't. It's not that we back away completely, but we don't come anywhere near serving Him completely either. We just don't seem to get it, even after all He's done for us. We keep Him at arms-length, when His arms were stretched out on the cross for us. We want Jesus; just don't ask us to do anything. Where is the excitement and enthusiasm about being a committed, passionate, and faithful servant? Something's wrong with this picture. The pain of life is so very real. We cry out for relief and deliverance, and He hears us and answers us. Yet, we feel very little when it comes to the weak, the vulnerable, the broken, and the crushed who have fallen by the wayside. When do we cry out for them in their anguish and agony and run to wipe their tears?

At first, I totally missed the big picture, that the church has lost its soul. With the guidance of the Holy Spirit I began to figure it out. It was at my first parish, St. Paul, Shobonier, in rural central Illinois, where my thoughts about the church began to emerge in fits and spurts. Then, there was a jump in awareness and my sermons did take on a tone that was more challenging. Observing the struggles we were going through in our denomination at that time added another level of awareness. Then, more recently, it hit me, and my awareness grew exponentially, startled me, terrified me. I saw the dynamic operative throughout the whole church.

What also has to be said, admitted, and confessed, is that as my awareness increased, so did my eagerness to be sure there was a corresponding increase in the degree to which I responded to the call to sacrifice. It's not like my wife and I weren't always responsible, frugal, sacrificial stewards, and willing servants. We never had that much, but we managed well and experienced an abundance of blessing along the way. Even though all we signed on for was a modest, simple life, we have accumulated a net worth far beyond anything we could have imagined.

All the way along, however, I experienced the internal conflict and tension of trying to let go of our resources, to not be so attached to the material things of this world "where moth and rust doth corrupt" (Matthew 6:19, KJV). My giving was always done grudgingly. For many years, I didn't find joy in making a sacrificial gift. Not only had I made an inaccurate assessment of the effectiveness of the church as it was about its mission, I also missed the full experience of thankfulness and joy in response to all that Christ had done for me. It was incredible. I had missed the very center of what my faith is all about. Yet, there were those lingering concerns about having enough to provide for the family, the education of our children, and having some resources saved for retirement and nursing care. There were my own insecurities as a person. Whatever is in the mix of issues related to being a good steward of what God has given me to manage for a while, I felt at times like He was prying it out of my clenched fist. I was holding on tight, while preaching that others should be cheerful givers. I was not always a cheerful giver; I understand what that's like.

My hope is that we will no longer repress, deny, or distort the truth about ourselves, but rather see ourselves for whom and what we are. It is only when the truth is acknowledged that we can have good conversation with God, and, with the help of the Holy Spirit, make good decisions. Are we going to make a conscious decision to continue to go with the flow in the river of cultural tradition or consider making some changes? Unless we see and accept ourselves for whom and what we are, we will never claim the abundant life that God wants for us all, namely, the life of a disciple that satisfies the heart and is the path to peace.

It is my fervent hope and prayer that Christians will be different. The inspiration and motivation generated by the promises of forgiveness and eternal life in Christ have the potential to be life changing. The never-failing love of a God who always forgives can be transformational, a beautiful and gentle invitation to grow.

Christians hear Jesus' call to submission, surrender, and compassionate service, and experience the tremendous tension it generates in our lives. We ask for forgiveness without an awareness of the seriousness and gravity of our request. Then, one day, we are stunned by the full impact of our disobedience. We are not charitable, generous, or compassionate people. Not even close. We realize that we have been trying to finesse a way to combine our affection for what this world has to offer with our loyalty to Christ. Now we get what Jesus meant when He said in Luke 16:13 (NIV), "You can't serve both God and money." Overwhelmed by the awareness that He forgives us for far more than we were ever aware, the call to a life of obedience sounds totally different. His burden is easy and His yoke is light.

"The Gospel call is one for radical change [. . .]   Jesus Christ [. . .] caused scandal almost everywhere he went. Christianity is a religion whose founder was killed because he challenged people to get up out of their comfortable ways, [. . .] and to start living real charity."[76] Our response appears to be that basically we see ourselves as good people, and for now, that's enough. In so doing, we give evidence of a hardness of heart that has not been broken.

We don't seem to be concerned about how the management of our financial resources impacts the millions who are suffering, abandoned, starving, and living in squalor with little sense of dignity or hope. All the while, we are deceptively giving the impression of being what we are not. Nothing is going to change until we stop repressing, denying, and distorting the truth about ourselves. The heartbreaking and painful truth is that, for all practical purposes, with the exception of those close to us, we really don't care all that much about anyone else. We don't care about the fallout that results from decisions we make in the form of sins of omission. While it sounds almost inhuman to say that we don't care who we hurt, it is the truth. It is a picture of what we are really like.

When confronted with this image of ourselves, we pull back in shock and stunned silence. "Wait a minute. What did you say? Who are you talking about? You didn't mean that? We're not like that." Tragically, that's exactly what I said and what I meant. This is the way God sees us. We need to be honest with ourselves and own the truth – no airbrushing, no touch-ups, and no photo-shopping.

So how can I do right by my wife and kids, while not forgetting about the well-being of others? Providing for those in our family is a commitment that we make when we get married; this is foundational – a covenant responsibility. Without question, we also need to ask whether we are being cold, cruel, and indifferent if somebody in another family is starving to death and we do nothing, even though we could. It is not right to make sure my kids get to the doctor when needed, but sit idly by when there is a child in another family who doesn't have access to medical care. Within the framework of our economic circumstances and pursuit of the American Dream, we have to ask how our decisions impact the well-being of others. While we may not be guilty of crass materialism, we cling to a middle class lifestyle, remaining largely indifferent to the needs and well-being of others. All the while, we maintain the deception that allows us to remain cloaked in the mantle of respectability.

Coming to the awareness that my life is a moral desert, an ethical wasteland, has been very painful. It is only by God's grace that I find peace. It is a struggle for all of us to live in the tension between good and evil, right and wrong, selfishness and selflessness, indifference and compassion, and accumulating and sharing. Each of us has to look into our own hearts, asking the Holy Spirit to guide the soul-searching and grant us insight.

A re-evaluation of the stewardship of our time and financial resources is probably not an item on our "to-do" list. It's not something we want to deal with. We don't even want to think about the possibility that we have adopted a minimum standard for evaluating whether we are disciples or not. We're more likely to say something like, "I've found my comfort zone with stewardship, one that fits quite comfortably with the lifestyle I have chosen. So don't upset me with these idealistic principles and suggest that I give and serve just enough to be able to convince myself I'm caring, compassionate, and charitable. Don't ask me to do any soul searching about how I manage my financial resources and use my time. I may have to find a church that 'understands.'" I wish I saw it differently, but I don't want to get my hopes up that much of anything will change.

In our hearts, we have this uneasy feeling. On some level, we realize that we don't even come close to measuring up to the biblical standard. Our attempts to rationalize and justify don't cut it. Deep down, we know that there is immense suffering in the world, that there is so much poverty and need, and yet we are cold and indifferent. Occasionally, the words come back to us, "How many times can a man turn his head and pretend that he just doesn't see? The answer my friend, is blowin' in the wind. The answer is blowin' in the wind" (Bob Dylan, *"Blowin' in the* Wind," 1962.). After a few moments, we are able to resist the stirrings of the Holy Spirit and ready to move on. It's tough to own and confess that we are not as generous, caring, compassionate, and charitable as we think we are.

We are caught up in the age-old struggle against the strangle-hold the world has on us. We are attached to the prosperous life of the 21st century world, and we're not willing to let go of stuff and commit ourselves totally to the Lord and the mission of the Church. Our hearts do not seem to be touched by, and we do not seem to be worried about, sharing the Gospel, let alone about suffering, poverty, inequality, and exploitation.

Rather than appreciating the abundance of blessings we receive from the hand of our good and gracious God, we start thinking our life could be better.

We believe we are entitled to happiness on our own terms [. . .] cobbling together a list of the "greatest hits" of the things [others have]. As we do so, we implicitly tell God, and ourselves, that what we have simply is not enough. We misunderstand the value of our present state, and in turn, we fail to see the goodness of the process by which God is leading us into the future.[77]

We are not satisfied with what has already been given, the gift of His Son, who suffered and died on the cross so that we can have forgiveness and eternal life. We convince ourselves that what we have will not make us happy. We grapple with the urgency of accumulation in pursuit of a happiness that is only a temporary illusion. There is more to life.

Couldn't we all be disciples who practice simplicity and frugality? By so doing, we would be better positioned to meet the needs of those living in poverty, the suffering, the abandoned, and the destitute. Yes, we need a job to provide for our households and pay the bills. At the same time, we need to be concerned about the malnourished, displaced refugees, the homeless, and kids with no access to health care. Concern for our own family and our personal challenges does not absolve us from being concerned for the poor and disadvantaged. After providing for the needs of our household, we are there for others; this is what discipleship is about. I offer it to us as a model that can serve as a baseline when evaluating how we're doing as disciples. The lifestyle I'm describing is essential for those on the journey to spiritual maturity. "But if anyone has the world's goods and sees his brother in need, and yet closes his heart against him, how does the love of God abide in him" I John 3:17. When Christ comes into our lives, everything changes. The life of discipleship is so much more than anything we could have imagined.

It can't be stated strongly enough that the change described is a daily struggle that can only be sustained with the help of the Holy Spirit. We need to be reading the Bible every day. We need to be praying for guidance in our decision making many times a day. We need to be in a Bible class. We need to be faithful in attending worship with our congregation. These are some of the important ways in which we find the strength to walk with the Lord as His disciples.

Chapter 11

The Church: Insignificant, Irrelevant, and Marginalized

The famous words of the poem "Maud Muller," by John Greenleaf Whittier, are a fitting description of the church: "For all sad words of tongue or pen, the saddest are these: 'It might have been!'" Members would certainly not intentionally do anything to weaken, harm, undermine, sabotage, or destroy the church. We don't realize that's exactly what we are doing.

What Might Have Been

The new reality is that we are but a shadow of what we once were, and that we ourselves had more than just a little to do with the decline. We contributed to it directly, through our less than inspiring witness as disciples who did not fulfill our calling. It's time to accept responsibility for our demise and stop making excuses by blaming the culture for the moral decline which has resulted in a disregard for biblical teaching. Many of our members tell us, "The collapse of cultural moral standards in our country needs to be called out. We don't preach about it in our sermons the way we used to. The world is going to hell in a hand-basket. Sin is no longer called sin. What's needed is a good dose of hellfire and brimstone for them there sinners out there. We have to deal with it." They are convinced that this is precisely the action we Christians need to take in order to give an effective witness.

The sad reality is that we can't. We have zero credibility. The world's perception of us is all negative. Therefore, any effort to deal with it is only going to make us appear to be even more hypocritical. Given the state of the church, why would anyone listen to our witness? Why would anyone care about our views? Why would anyone be sympathetic to our cause? What plagues the church today is not the significant changes in the ethics, morals, and values of our culture, threats to religious liberty, or the assertion that the divinity of Jesus (the core of Christian theology) was first conceived of by his followers. No, the millstone around our neck is our abandonment of the biblical call to discipleship. Giving priority and attention to the moral climate of our culture serves as a distraction and smokescreen. We lose sight of the bigger issue, addressing the challenges posed by materialism, consumerism, the good life, the American Dream, and their effect on our understanding of discipleship and the witness we give.

It is of paramount importance to keep in mind what the culture thinks of the church. How does the world see us? What does the world think of us? They see us as rigid, inflexible, and so narrow-minded and "far right" that they feel they can't even have a conversation with most of us in the church. They see us as having erected a barrier around us that makes it hard for them to connect with us. So why should they even waste their time trying to explain to us how they see us, and what they think of us. Basically, they have written us off. They see us as preaching to the choir - playing to our base, if you will. They would like us to at least act like grown-ups who realize that we can begin by trying to understand each other. In some ways, they are correct, and in some ways, they are not. In some cases, they unfairly label us as intolerant, and in some ways, they are right on. Where does that leave us? How can we reach out to them? How can we try to develop a relationship with them?

We can begin by owning the problem and accepting responsibility for the decline of the church, rather than moan, groan, gripe, and complain about how we are besieged by our culture. Then, we can act like grown-ups who realize it is our responsibility to be sure we are always ready to listen to others, and be sure we are the ones making the effort to understand them. It is always our responsibility to understand the other. Expecting folks to understand us is a recipe for disaster.

Then, let's confess that we have precious little ethical or moral standing on which to base our witness. Let's acknowledge that our cumulative record of sacrificial service as a church does not inspire or influence in a way that would result in others being interested in who we are and what we are about. We can admit that, given the way we live, our religion doesn't mean much to us. Even Jesus doesn't mean much to us. Why should it mean anything to others?

The people we are trying to reach can justifiably say to us, "You're not all that different from everybody else. What right do you have to tell us how we are to live our lives? Your walk has not validated your talk. You've got a lot of nerve to think you can tell us what is right and what is wrong, how to live our lives, and what morals need to be legislated so we are forced to live by them." We come off as self-righteous, hypocritical, and "holier than thou." We have lost what little credibility we had left.

So how do we, as the clergy, encourage taking up the challenge to revisit important elements in our belief system? Even if we say it in a nice way, in a way that conveys patience, gentleness, and understanding, members will really get upset. How can we be painfully truthful and honest, without them really getting ticked off? No matter how carefully we say it, we quickly cross the threshold of threat to their current beliefs, which in turn triggers a backlash. Those who get it will understand. Those who don't get it will find fault with what we have to say no matter how hard we try to say it with tact and love.

We just have to be real! The church is a heart-breaking disappointment to God. There are times when, without intention or awareness, it comes close to being a fraud. What percentage of a congregation's offerings are used to maintain the congregation and how much is used for outreach mission, service, and charity. When we find that a disproportionate amount is being used to operate the congregation, there is a good chance we've got a problem. This is where stewardship education can also be problematic, sometimes misleading, and even deceptive.

Now, more than ever, the church has the potential to be and do so much more. In a time of unprecedented wealth, the church has sadly fallen so far short of its potential as to bring God to tears. This isn't the first time it has happened. In Old Testament times, God was stricken with grief when his people forgot about him. They forgot about all He had done for them and forgot their promises to be His emissary, as a light to the nations. They said, "All that the Lord has spoken, we will do" (Exodus 19:8). However, they didn't follow through. God was distraught. Now the people of God, in both the Old and New Testaments, have been unfaithful.

Even in the hills of Kentucky near Barrymore, where small town folks are struggling to survive, they are blessed beyond measure compared to the standard of living of billions in the world. Most of the rest of us are doing so much better than they are, and we wonder, how does God see us? This marvelous community we call the Holy Christian Church has squandered its capital, its status, its potential, and whatever measure of respect it once had.

What reality are we living in? We live in a reality of our own making. We are oblivious to what the Scriptures teach about what it means to be disciples in the church. We haven't even noticed how far we have strayed from what God wants us to be. We don't have a clue that God is inconsolable in his grief. It's hard for Him to even look at us and accept the magnitude of our betrayal and ingratitude. Thankfully, by grace, He does. It's hard for Him to think about what has happened. It is almost inconceivable. It is beyond belief. He hasn't given any indication of a successor community here on earth, as was promised to the Old Testament community of faith. God is stuck with us. Then, I remember His promise to work all things for good. This is the only reason it is even possible to continue to be His presence in the world, loving and serving others.

Where is the abundance of compassion? We just don't see it. We always hope the story ends well. However, the way events are unfolding, this one will not. A big part of the reason is what we have done to ourselves. Oh, sure, there are those in the church who blame our decline on moral issues, political issues, and the biases of science. If only it were that simple. The truth is, we have brought this decline on ourselves. What we have done to ourselves has had a far greater impact that what has been going on in the world around us. Our wounds are self-inflicted. It will be the supreme irony and greatest tragedy of all time if the reason our story doesn't end well is because of what we have done to ourselves.

The heyday of Christianity and its subsequent decline have been going on since the late 1960's and early 1970's. Until then, church membership, attendance, and offerings continued at levels where churches and their leaders were comfortable, pleased, and satisfied; this provided cover, a smoke-screen for a cancer that was leading to decay, decline, and irrelevance. Until that time, church membership remained in the mainstream of American family life.

The 1960's and 1970's saw the beginning of a substantial shift from mainline churches to evangelical, non-denominational, and community churches. Members of traditional denominations began to migrate to churches whose beliefs weren't all that different from what they grew up with in a traditional denomination. People often changed churches because they didn't experience the passion and excitement of a community on fire for the Lord, and they didn't understand why. The just knew they wanted more. This shift isn't a bad thing. It is good that they responded to the malaise and opted for an energy and enthusiasm that gave them hope.

This hope, however, also soon faded. What happened? Perhaps more precisely, what didn't happen is that while we developed a more modern and expressive worship style where the music was more attuned to a younger generation, and there was a warm, welcoming, friendly atmosphere, these outward forms were not accompanied by a commitment to live out an uncompromised understanding of what it means to be a disciple. They didn't get it either. This trend only served to slightly slow the decline of the church. It may have actually served as another smoke-screen that hid the seriousness and gravity of what was happening, and still is. We have yet to come to terms with it. The "Nones" have increased to 30 percent of the population. The story isn't going to end well, and we will stand there with our mouths open – stunned, shaken, and puzzled, and asking, "What happened?"

Praying, meditating, and reflecting on all of this has led me back to a biblical perspective that explains the decline. It doesn't take all that much to figure it out. We know what the Scriptures teach, but we ignore it like the plague. We want no part of it. It's like we really don't want to see it. We want to remain in denial. If we see it, grasp it, and acknowledge it, then just maybe the power of the Holy Spirit will challenge us to do something about it. We just might feel compelled to live out the biblical model of discipleship. As long as the status quo allows me to rationalize and justify what I'm doing as a Christian leader or lay person, I'm good with that. I really don't want to upset the applecart. We're ok with the way things are as long as the status quo of moral decline and perceived cultural attacks on religion provide the cover that allows us to repress, deny, and avoid the real issue. We're perfectly content. There's no reason to get all bent out of shape about it. What's the big deal? The big deal is that the church continues to decline, we are unable to reach as many people with the "Good News," and the army of faithful servants needed to serve the suffering in the world remains on the sidelines.

We've Lost Our Seat at the Table

The church continues to be tolerated by the government because it helps to establish the moral compass of our nation, which contributes to the overall good order and the well-being of society. The church gets only a modest amount of respect from politicians of all stripes the government, and most of that capital has now been spent. The world lets us do our thing, but we've lost our seat at the table. We are little more than window dressing.

While there are a few faithful men and women who, moved by the Holy Spirit working through the Word, repent and are eager to reform their lives and walk more closely in accord with God's will and ways, for all intents and purposes, all that remains of the local congregation is a place that will serve us when it's time for a wedding, a hospital call, or a funeral. In many instances, congregational life doesn't move far beyond pastoral care. We don't want a life of sacrifice and service as part of the deal. A growing number of people have no church affiliation at all. They don't turn to the church for anything.

Looking at the sorry state of the church today – its ineffectiveness, futility, and decline - is heartbreaking, especially considering the unlimited and untapped potential that could be realized if the community of believers were living lives of sacrifice and service. In the big scheme of things, the church has become irrelevant. It lacks the passionate commitment to mission and discipleship needed to give it credibility. We are entering the modern dark ages of a declining church that is marginalized and insignificant.

Is there any chance that a response of loving service to our communities and the world could be carried out together without denominational self-interest? I want to believe there is, but it just isn't going to happen. We would have to get past the point where we engage in theological debate about who interprets the Bible correctly and who has the right teachings. We, as the church, are in a struggle to retain whatever credibility we have left as a place of mercy and compassion. Getting our act together collectively is beyond the scope of what I see as a reasonable expectation. While there may be a few pockets of renewal and revival, there's not going to be a ground-swell of change. We are beyond redemption. As He did with the Old Testament children of Israel, God has just about written us off.

In the grand sweep of history, we are in danger of becoming no more than an asterisk. We, as God's people, became little more than a footnote once before. Our gracious and loving Father gave us another chance when He sent His Son to gather to Himself a new Israel, the church. It happened once. It's not going to happen again.

Our current record of service is a disgrace. We are stumbling around in the wilderness of materialism, self-interest, the pursuit of the American Dream, and the good life. Having forgotten the essence of who we are, we have abdicated any legitimate claim to be worthy of respect. We have almost totally abandoned our status as trustees of love, hope, and promise.

We have lost whatever moral authority we once had. People hear us share the Gospel and stand there flabbergasted at the audacity of folks who labor under the illusion they have enough moral standing to think that anybody should listen to them. The church has lost its way, lost its identity, and lost its soul.

Does the church do much good? Does the church help many people? Does the church show an abundance of mercy and compassion? Does the church save many souls? Not really. The church doesn't come anywhere near realizing its potential. In so many ways, it has been a huge disappointment. No! It has been a monumental failure. Christians living the lives of dedicated disciples could make an unimaginable and unprecedented difference, but they don't. We have become insignificant, irrelevant, and marginalized. In the eyes of the community, our image and reputation are viewed as not much different from community service organizations like the Kiwanis, the Rotary Club, the Lions Club, or a Go-Fund-Me project on Facebook. We are seen as no different from others in the community who volunteer and help as mentors, coaches, and tutors for the less fortunate.

All of this is so sad and so unnecessary. The world looks at us as if we are crazy and not just because our beliefs are viewed as superstition, fable, or mythology. They look at us and say, "Are you nuts? You don't live in accordance with your own teachings, and you want us to listen to you and give consideration to what you believe? You want us to adopt your views about ethics, morals, and values?" We have to understand that this is the way many in the world see us. This has to be a foundational presupposition. If we read it any differently, we will scratch our heads and our hearts will break as we wonder why the church is going down the tubes, and how we missed it. We need to accept the reality of the ways of the world as a given, instead of expending energy in trying to defend ourselves and change the world in ways that only alienate us further.

Anno Domini, the Year of Our Lord 2017

Jesus is the very center of history. The year of His birth is recognized as the fulcrum by which time in the Western world is measured. Reading the Journal Sentinel, on January 1, 2017, it was apparent that there is almost a total disconnect between the church and what is happening in the world. In a summary of the year in review, there were stories about a renewal of the nuclear arms race, terrorism, immigration, gun violence, homelessness, and education. There was nothing about the church. Even on the Sunday before the 500th anniversary of the Reformation, on October 31, 2017, there were only two articles about it in the Journal Sentinel, even though Milwaukee and Wisconsin are traditional strongholds of Lutheranism in the U.S. There was no news about any huge impact the church had on the world. There wasn't any news about anything happening in the church.

The church has the potential to be "the story" almost every day. Even when there are big national or international developments, there should be some exciting or inspiring story about how the church is involved in sacrificial service. The One Holy Christian Apostolic Church on earth has the potential and resources to give an awesome witness and exert its influence in the world in a way that today seems unimaginable and impossible. Jesus grew up and asked us to follow him on the path to loving, sacrificial service – giving our all for him and showing our love for Him by loving each other in human family. When recapping 2016 and making projections for 2017, the Journal-Sentinel never mentions the church. This omission speaks volumes. All we find is the muted voice of the Pope with his annual first of the year message, which included prayers for peace and encouragement to help the poor.

The way to heaven passes through the poor urban neighborhoods in our cities, the slums of Calcutta, those living in impoverished villages in Africa, and refugee camps in the Middle-East. It passes through anywhere we find poverty, starvation, and suffering, wherever we see those who are disenfranchised, victimized, and marginalized. By serving these people, our light could be shining brightly in a dark world. We could be the number one story of the year, every year. We could be the *Time* "person" of the year, every year.

Some of us are extremely disheartened about the church's prospects for the future. We are devastated by its impotence, distraught by its irrelevance, and in despair that it never became what it could have been. The history of the church seems more like a modern Greek tragedy than an account of a dynamic community of servants who give their all to our Lord Jesus in loving service and sacrifice. I remember participating in a group exercise at a training workshop, where we were told to gather in two concentric circles facing each other. Then, we were assigned a phrase. As the circles moved in opposite directions, we had a chance to experience what it was like when the people in the other circle would say with inflection and feeling: "You're a threat," "You're a possibility," or "You're irrelevant." It was a powerful, moving experience.

The church no longer has much of a chance of even being a possibility. God tried to get through to His people many times in the Old Testament, and finally went to "Plan B," which involved exile, a remnant, and a chance to start over. "Plan B" hasn't gone well either, especially recently. We need to pray, reflect and ask why. It is a function of living out our lives as Christians in a way that we look pretty much like everybody else. There is not much reason to be hopeful that much will change within the community of believers, and there is no "Plan C."

Spiritual nurture and charitable service are surely treasures to those who receive them. Those who have heard the Gospel of Jesus Christ have been truly blessed with a peace that passes all understanding. Those who have been forgotten and fallen by the wayside are thankful for the loving service rendered to them and for any help they receive. It means everything to them in their daily struggle just to survive.

The dark side of the church is that we have done so very little when compared to our potential. Discipleship, especially looking out for the needs of others, hasn't been lifted up as a high-priority concern, and that threatens the viability of the church. We are all smoke and mirrors and ought to be horrified by our heartless response. Until we face up to what's going on, nothing will change, and there isn't a chance we will move past it. The way it stands now, we don't have a clue. The church has left its mark by the conspicuous absence of acts of charity, love, and mercy to which we are called as disciples. This is how we are identified. This is the mark we have left. This is the lasting impression we have given the world.

The church is oblivious to how its image and credibility have impacted the effectiveness of its outreach and mission. We just don't get it. Based on our traditional role in society and the world, we are out of touch with reality in regards to our relevance. We just assume that our status is as it once was, that we have the capacity to influence, and that we still have a big role on the world stage. The truth is we are part of the supporting cast. We are perilously close to just having nothing more than a bit part, and being one of the names we don't pay attention to when the credits run.

Basically, the church is doing a good job of playing to its base and spinning its message to make ourselves look better than we are. We weren't even aware that this is what we were doing. We looked good when we measured ourselves by the standards we set for ourselves. We don't look so good when we measure ourselves by God's standards. We are doomed to being relegated to insignificance and irrelevance by our own mistakes, and there is no reason to think we are going to change. Why? First, changing would necessitate rattling too many cages and rocking too many boats. Second, most of us are content with the way things are. And, remember, it is the world that has to change.

We've Already Lost the Culture Wars

A massive shift in the subterranean, tectonic, cultural plates has produced a spiritual earthquake of proportions that has only taken place a few times in the long history of the church. We've already lost the culture wars! We've already lost the culture! This understanding is key! This fact has to become a presupposition for all decisions about how to best give witness. To do otherwise will result in well-intentioned actions that turn out to be counter-productive. Cultural values have changed. While some in the church see it differently, there is not much we can do. The question is, how do we give witness in this new reality? When we come up with that answer, we will also have found the way to teach a mature understanding of this issue and develop an approach that will do exactly what we want in terms of retaining our youth and attracting new members.

With the Spirit's guidance and strength, our hope is to live such exemplary lives that people sit up, take notice and want to explore why it is that we live lives of sacrificial service. We need to be identified by love and compassion. Our whole being, as individuals, and our whole purpose, as Christian families, needs to be focused on ministry to the poor, visiting the sick, clothing the naked, and feeding the hungry. As saints and disciples, we need to stand out so that others see our total commitment to the unmet needs of others. We want to follow Christ's command to love one another, letting those we serve learn, by our lives and actions, how much we care for them. Then, they will begin to ask why it is that we live as we do, and we can answer with what we believe. "Before being elected Pope, Francis gave a speech to his fellow Cardinals warning against becoming a 'self-preferential' church, rather than one that goes out of itself into the margins of society to be with those who suffer. That is where God is working in the world and where He calls us to be. As Pope Paul VI once said: 'Modern man listens more willingly to witnesses than to teachers.' Francis loves that phrase."[78]

If those we are trying to reach stumble because of the offense of the cross and the call to discipleship, that's one thing: "For the message of the cross is foolishness to those who are perishing, but to those of us who are being saved it is the power of God" (I Cor. 1:18). The cross is enough of a stumbling block. We certainly don't want to add other hurdles that are imposed rather than scriptural. As I see it, that is exactly what we are doing when we misapply our theology. Those who hear the Gospel also have to deal with the stumbling blocks of the Trinity, Jesus being both true God and true man, the six day creation, Noah and the flood, Jonah being swallowed by the whale, and miracles. Stumbling blocks are also encountered by those who are struggling with their faith due to pain, suffering, tragedy, or misfortune, and have questions about why these things happen and where God fits into the picture. Why are we adding another, namely, uninspiring witness resulting from a compromised understanding of discipleship?

The Church in an Alternative Reality

We have changed our reality, our world view, and the conceptual framework by which we order our lives. The world lives in one reality, while we remain in a bubble we have created for ourselves. We live in two different worlds. Living within our own reality, we think we're a whole lot more relevant than we are. We are also living under the illusion that we remain true to our mission. Finding examples of the selfless life of sacrificial service is like looking for a needle in a haystack. All of this is so tragic because the church has the potential to be so much more than it is. It helps explain why the church isn't a player and doesn't have a seat at the table. We are clinging to the erroneous assumption that we are imperfect yet viable, significant, and influential, a force to be reckoned with. We are nowhere near a player in the doings and happenings in the world. That role has long passed us by. The church is moving as if it were in an altered state of consciousness under the influence of LSD, having an exaggerated sense of our importance and ability to influence. In reality, we have become irrelevant.

God has chosen us as His bride and entered into a covenant relationship with us. We have committed ourselves to be faithful to Him and to serve Him with all of our being. The marriage began with a tremendous sense of destiny and confidence in the power of the resurrection. There remains a grass-roots conviction that we are faithfully obeying Him, when in reality, this is a false confidence that exists only in our convoluted reasoning based on an inaccurate understanding of what we want the church to be. We are quick to assert that we have been called out as disciples to serve His purposes, and that surely He will bring His purposes to fruition through us. We have become quite set in our ways, thin skinned, and ready at the drop of a hat to take on and defend our beliefs whenever they are challenged. It's almost like we're saying, "Come one! Challenge me! Ask me anything you want." It almost sounds like we want to be challenged. We are living as an argument, rather than living as His story.

Actually, the world doesn't need our permission. Besides, any questions, concerns, and issues they may have had were answered long ago. Our life of compromised discipleship was all the answer they needed. The dynamic core of who we were has given way to a church that is only a shadow of its former self. We have to come to terms with the possibility that for some time we have been living in an alternate reality, while a pluralistic and secularized world has moved on.

We labor under the illusion of our own importance, significance, and relevance. We live with the assumption that we are something that we are not. Someone would have to snap their fingers to bring us out of our trance, resume life in the real world, regain our sense of mission, reclaim our commitment to share the Gospel, and reemphasize the importance of serving those in need. Until then, our well-intentioned efforts, and our sincere desire to live as Christ's witnesses are not going to be effective. We are not going to be the blessing to others that we fervently hope and pray we will be. As much as we want to share Jesus with others, our sincere efforts will be rendered ineffective and irrelevant by the imaginary world we have created in our dream-like existence, which has become the construct that frames meaning for us.

We have declined into insignificance and irrelevance and are becoming more than just a disappointment. We have become comfortable with the accommodation we have made with our culture. We are far more unworthy of grace than we have ever been. Now, at a time, place, and circumstance when Christians cumulatively have an abundance of resources and the potential to be known far and wide as irrationally exuberant, wildly vibrant, compassionate, committed, and sacrificial servants, we are a tragic disappointment. We have been seduced into a trance by the materialism and consumerism that are the mantras of our culture. Did we plan for this to happen? No. Did we want this to happen? No. Nevertheless, this is where we are. Using "holy smoke and mirrors," the church has redefined discipleship, compromised the Gospel, and lost its soul. The painful truth is that we can write off the church as an effective instrument for sharing the saving Gospel of Jesus Christ in any significant, meaningful way, let alone for it to become a powerful and vibrant instrument of the Holy Spirit.

We've also painted ourselves into a corner. If we make a significant course correction in our ministry plan, we risk losing many of our current members. We've taught them well. They have joined us precisely because we offer the brand of Christianity they want. They like the idea of being members of a low-expectation church. Our members want help and comfort in times of trial and tribulation, and we clergy are there to provide it - as it should be. The laity know what they want from their clergy: comfort in times of trouble and somebody to marry and bury. They do not want bold, prophetic preaching about the biblical teaching of discipleship that results in our standing out in stark contrast to our culture. Discipleship must include a rejection of the American Dream and the principles that define the culture's definition of all that is involved in the "good life."

However, when the biblical understanding of discipleship is taught, and the way gets difficult, we look for "an opening through the trees that promises a softer, easier path. Distracted and diverted, [we] slip off and never return."[79] Whatever decline we experience in membership, attendance, and offerings is being spun in a way that we don't have to take any of the responsibility.

The decline of the church, an institution with almost unlimited potential for blessing, is quite possibly the saddest and most tragic development in all of history. There is as great a need for forgiveness as there has ever been. In as great an expression of love and mercy as we can imagine, that forgiveness is there for us, offered fully and freely through the suffering, death, and resurrection of Jesus Christ.

We've been in a state of denial about what has been happening in the church for a long time. We have avoided the truth. We've rationalized how the world sees us. We need to face it, and own it. The world's perception of us is spot on. We have attempted to compensate, trying to make it appear as if we are vibrant and alive, when in reality that is so far from the truth.

Figuring out that the foundation upon which we have built our life is crumbling is devastating. Becoming aware that our life is spiritually bankrupt is a life shattering experience. Yet, we're still here.

Then, we hear the Gospel and are reassured that God is still here for us too, and the healing begins. We can regain the confidence that, in Christ, there is hope and a future. The rest will all come together. We are already down the road in our search for how to live out our vocation. From that point on, we will be at peace. All of the unrealistic expectations about how we were going to grow the congregation are stripped away. We live a simple life of sacrifice and service, and touch as many people as we can with the love of Christ. Our meaning in life is found in being Christ to our neighbor.

While the church now only touches on the fringes of its essence, the clarion call to discipleship still rings out, and invites us to participate in the joyous response to all that Christ has done for us. We welcome those who are seeking the meaning of it all to join us. We welcome them into a church that has a dismal record of compassion. We welcome them to join in the exploration of all of the meaning that is packed into Galatians 5:6, "the faith that finds its expression in love is all that matters."

Unless we, as the church, do some honest reflection and repent, we will continue to be our own worst enemy, and will continue to decline. At this point, however, even our best efforts aren't going to have much of an impact and make much of a difference. We will make the effort anyway. This is what we do! This is who we are! We will repurpose ourselves through a reconceptualization of our mission and a reordering of our priorities.

Chapter 12

Where Do We Go from Here?

What happens next? What happens when we realize the church has become irrelevant? Maybe someone will be guided by the Holy Spirit to see how we can pick up the pieces and lead us once again down the path to healing and wholeness. Is it still possible to find a way to turn things around and move forward as the church? That's not going to happen. It's too late.

Of course there will always be a small number of the faithful who, as individuals and groups moved by the Holy Spirit working through the Word, will repent, and eagerly, willingly, and joyfully reform their lives and walk more closely in accord with God's will and ways. These exceptions are the devoted church workers, clergy, laity, and missionaries who give their all in faithful devotion. However, the cumulative impact of their witness will not be enough to change the world's impression and image of the church. The small number who do respond to the Gospel will simply be viewed as a tiny sect within the larger church. Our better angels are few and far between. All we can do is seek the Holy Spirit's strength and guidance as we move forward on a personal level and in a few small groups. The church is still an instrument of God's purpose, albeit a dim shadow of what it was called to be, an entity that has lost its soul.

God has called us to himself, and we pray that in time, God will draw us to the discovery of our path forward as individuals. For most of us, living out our lives in a manner consistent with what the Bible teaches about discipleship will require a radical change in our lifestyle. It calls for a major shift in our thinking, and major modifications in the way we are used to doing things, a transformation. From the moment we awake in the morning, everything is viewed through a new filter. Everything is seen differently. It does not mean we neglect our primary commitments to relationships, job, or school, but the framework that gives meaning to all of these commitments, and in which they are all lived out, will most certainly change. It means that Jesus becomes our very reason for being. Living out the mandate of the Gospel is what gives meaning to all of life. Decisions and choices are made in the context of living according to His will. It means that life becomes a totally different experience.

We need to be specific about what this means. As I see it, there are only a very few who are doing what He has asked. Here is what we look like. We awake in the morning with the specific intent to represent Him and serve Him as best we can, in absolutely everything we do. We embrace the call to discipleship, and the mandate for love and caring, and for self-denial and service. We live in humble submission to a Lord who gave His all for us, brought us into a close personal relationship with Him, and calls us to walk with Him and follow in His steps.

Guided and strengthened by the Holy Spirit, we will aspire to live out the biblical understanding of discipleship. The future can be crystal clear. As for me personally, while I'm distraught about the future of the church, I'm ecstatic about my personal future as a Christian. While reality is terribly painful, my confusion and spiritual struggles have been resolved. I'm no longer troubled by them. I am at peace. It is with eager anticipation that I look forward to being able to walk down the road more faithfully in a life of humble service in the name of Jesus. While the opportunity for the whole church to be a powerful cumulative witness to the world has passed, the lives of passionate, sacrificial, self-giving Christians can be as meaningful and joyful as ever. Will the needed transformation of the church be realized? No! But having accepted reality, I can head on down the road, fully aware that like March in Wisconsin after a long winter, there all kinds of potholes out there.

What about our charitable contributions? Each of us can choose the ministries we will support financially and in which we will invest our precious volunteer time. Each of us can become partners in one or more of the arms of the church that we are excited about: mission work, mercy ministry, or education.

We can search for a congregation that comes closest to teaching and practicing biblical discipleship, one that would be open to praying for and asking for the help of the Holy Spirit in re-ordering their mission priorities. What might that look like? It would be one where they would be open to consider making it a budget priority to give away 25-40 percent or more of their offerings to missions and mercy ministry. It would be open to considering a provision in every fund raising campaign that would designate 25 percent of the campaign offering for mission, outreach, and mercy. It would have a standing resolution that 90 percent of bequests be given away to mission and mercy ministries selected by the congregation.

We need to seek out a congregation that is the source of our spiritual strength, a place where we share our faith, pray for, lift up, and encourage one another. It will be a healing community, where we are there for each other when we are hurting, broken, need support, or have made a mess of our lives. What a great place. However, what makes it extra special is that when nurtured and strengthened, we again become full partners in reaching out together in service to the community and the world, with all of the resources we can muster. The mission statement of the congregation might read: *In Christ - we gather for worship, care for each other, and serve our community.*

Deciding how to allocate our offerings is an exciting spiritual exercise. Trying to reach the point where we allocate 25-40 percent for ministry outside the congregation would be an exhilarating stage in our faith journey. What percentage of the offerings should we designate for the operating budget, including schools and high schools? What percentage should be allocated for mission, evangelism, outreach, and mercy ministry? Disciples resist the temptation to designate disproportionately high percentages of the offerings for home purposes. Disciples have moved beyond the point where we say, "We've got our own bills to pay."

For the average member who sees the local congregation as being there to meet their personal needs, this requires a tremendous, even radical, change in thinking, but it all starts with members experiencing life in a congregation which has a vibrant ministry and draws its thankfulness, joy, and compassion from their love for their Lord, who gave His all for them on the cross.

What if one of the foundational policies for seeking members to start a new congregation is the commitment to give away 25-40 percent of the offerings to ministry outside of the congregation, outreach, and the service of the poor, the vulnerable, the disadvantaged, and the needy? Realizing that we have to provide a salary for the pastor and rent a place to worship, would we be interested in becoming a part of the congregation? I posed the idea to some pastor friends over breakfast, and they were really enthusiastic about the idea. They thought "that's how the church was supposed to be." I have to fess up though, they were all retired.

It would be exciting and challenging to try to implement this policy in congregations with middle and upper income families who have an abundance of resources. These are the congregations that can do whatever they want because they have plenty of resources. They have plenty of help when someone is hurting in their congregation or community. What they usually don't have is nearly enough members who are willing to sacrifice to help the poor. If, under the preacher's leadership, a congregation is led to give away 25-40 percent, or more, of the offerings received to mission, charity, and outreach beyond their own church building and operating budget, then we have a congregation we can really get excited about. Find a congregation like that and we have found something special.

At the same time, I am deeply saddened by congregations that use almost all of their resources to make renovations or add an educational wing, fellowship space, or gym. We have to take a long and hard look at ourselves and our situations, before we make these kinds of decisions. Some are justified, and some are not.

A congregation needs to be nurtured spiritually and then moved on to the next level of discipleship as Rich Nathan did. Nathan is senior pastor of the Vineyard Church, a megachurch in Columbus, Ohio. He emphasized Jesus teachings about the poor (including getting to the root causes of poverty), peacemaking, and racial reconciliation. Rick Warren, well known Christian author, and pastor of the huge Saddleback Valley Community Church in Orange, California, "came up with a list of the five biggest problems on the planet: spiritual emptiness, self-serving leadership, poverty, pandemic disease, and illiteracy."[80] Then he developed the PEACE plan, PEACE being an acronym for Plant new churches, Equip servant leaders, Assist the poor, Care for the sick, and Educate the next generation. He was also estimated by Forbes to have earned $25 million. His practice of taking no salary from his church and giving a reverse tithe, that is giving 90 percent of his outside income away, is an outstanding practice of discipleship.

Warren hoped PEACE would involve ten million churches and a billion Christians, saying that:

a non-serving Christian is a contradiction. [...]With the Christian right still taking up all the oxygen in Washington, Warren began by saying that the first trend reporters should watch for was the return of the evangelicals to their nineteenth-century roots of 'compassionate activism.' Since the split in Protestantism, he explained, the mainline churches had tended to concern themselves with social morality – caring for the sick, poor, the dispossessed, and racial justice – while fundamentalists and evangelicals concerned themselves with personal morality and salvation. "But they really are all a part of the total Gospel – social justice, personal morality and salvation," he said. "And today a lot more [...] evangelicals are caring about those issues."[81]

Taking his PEACE plan as a case in point, he predicted that the embrace of such issues will lead to a second reformation. While the first was about beliefs and creeds, the second would be about deeds. His hope is that the second reformation would lead to a new spiritual awakening, a third Great Awakening in America, and the world.

When asked about his PEACE plan, Warren described how:

he had come to a turning point in his life two and a half years ago, when he read Psalm 72, wherein King Solomon prayed for more influence so he could support widows and orphans, care for the oppressed, and defend the defenseless. Warren had, he said, to repent to God for never having thought about the poor and the marginalized. "I've had four years of Greek and Hebrew and I've got doctorates. How did I miss the 2,000 verses in the Bible where it talks about the poor?"[82]

I rejoice in his discovery of these new scriptural insights, and fervently pray that his plan would succeed. It would be awesome if many congregations implemented his plan.

Dr. Joel Hunter, pastor of the nondenominational Northland Church in Orlando, Florida, adds another important dimension as a result of focusing on the Gospels more than the epistles of Paul.

The church, he said, relied too much on doctrine and not enough on the life of Christ – his ministry to the poor, the outcast, and the peacemakers. In 1996, when he felt the congregation was ready, he changed the emphasis of his preaching from individual faith and mutual service to service to the community as a whole. "He pushed us out" (one member said). "It's not a church that wants to gather you in [. . .] Sometimes [. . .] I do long for the 'holy huddle,' but it was the right thing to do."[83]

The passion and conviction of Nathan, Hunter, and Warren were not our first rodeos. These were not the first attempts at revival in the American church. There was "The Great Awakening" that occurred between the mid-1720s and the mid-1740s, where:

holiness was emphasized as a result of God's grace and one being born again. [. . .] It was George Whitfield (1715 - 1770), the Anglican preaching deacon and Methodist evangelist, who gave voice to this Great Awakening through his ardent [. . .] preaching tours. [. . .] He was an eloquent preacher, whose enthusiasm for the gospel resulted in a rapid spread of this Awakening.[84]

Another attempt to bring about the revival of the church known as the "second Great Awakening" began in 1801, when James McGready "emphasized the need to revive the spiritual lives of [. . .] frontier communities [. . .] in response to the steady secularizing of society and the rampant rationalism of the Enlightenment."[85]

The landscape changed with the industrial revolution (1860-1920), when the United States went from a largely agricultural nation to the leading industrial and manufacturing power in the world. More of the corporate gains were passed on to the industrial workers in the years following World War II. The American Dream was born and wages for white males increased until 1973 when they began to decline. Wages reached a plateau and were stable long enough for a large portion of the population to become part of what we now call the middle class. The wealth, comfort, and luxury we have enjoyed ever since is way beyond what life was like for average folk not many years before and became the essence of the American Dream. Efforts to bring about revival in the church are now jeopardized by our economic aspirations. This is not just an uphill battle; it's like trying to climb Denali, where only a few make it. There are few calls for the total commitment of a disciple. We usually go about ministry in the context of a comfortable lifestyle without being asked to consider self-denial as foundational in what it means to be a disciple.

Today the spiritual climate is totally different. The impact of the cultural challenge of the good life, the American Dream, the self-centered, self-serving, self-seeking lifestyles to which Christians also aspire, can't be understated. Is it possible that what is missing is a greater emphasis on biblical discipleship? Is it possible that the call to follow the scriptural mandate to live a life of self-denial and service needs to be stated much more emphatically?

"Time goes on, and the mission of the Roman Church will stand the test of time!" (Michael. J. D'augelli, "The God Squad," *Time*, July 3, 2017, 4.).[86] I'm suggesting that it hasn't and that, together with the whole church, it, too, has lost its soul. The quoted response speaks to an earlier article that touches on the importance of the Roman Church's positions on LGBTQ and birth control to the Church's Mission. The article mentions younger priests protesting at Black Lives Matter rallies, the wisdom of not preaching anti-abortion homilies, and providing opportunities for the community to address economic development, jobs, and food insecurity (Elizabeth Dias, "The God Squad," *Time*, June 19, 2018, 36-42.).[87] This is commendable and an important step forward. In addition, Pope Francis' continuing emphasis on a mission characterized by mercy has been added to the larger paradigm of ministry on the parish level. However, these changes in practice have not yet emphasized the over-arching framework into which these issues fit, namely, teaching and preaching a life of discipleship for the laity that is exemplified by sacrifice and service.

We can only make sense out of what is happening in the church when we realize and accept that its steep decline is a given. Then, having gained a sense of the big picture, we can decide how it is we want to be a part of the church. Any discussion of "the future" is limited to those individuals and congregations where there is a commitment to be disciples and a commitment to find others who want to be disciples with us. Without starting a movement, we can still find joy, peace, and purpose as part of a smaller group. Together, we will revise our schedules and routines, no longer participating in everything we did in the past. Exercise will be limited to what is needed for fitness. Facebook, TV, and Netflix will be limited in a manner consistent with an appropriate level of the need to stay connected. Then, we will find new ways and places to use our time, and serve in a manner consistent with our convictions.

We have those who aspire to be missionaries, pastors, teachers, and full time church workers. These folks have a heart for the Lord that doesn't quit. They are awesome and inspiring! They are joined by a relatively small percentage of the laity who are also excited to find a Christian fellowship that practices the biblical understanding of discipleship. People are looking for something to get excited about. People are looking for meaning and purpose. This is it! Let's give it to them.

Then, we have the overwhelming majority of members who are caught up in, and struggling with, finding the proper balance between the pursuit of the "American Dream" and a walk with the Lord as faithful disciples. Unfortunately, most of them are losing battle after battle, to the point where they are in danger of losing the war. We, as the church, have to prayerfully reflect upon the Scriptural vision of discipleship, considering whether, with the help of the Holy Spirit, we can aspire to a life of sacrificial service.

Be grounded in a denomination or religious expression and in a local congregation. Learn its teachings. Be in Bible study regularly. Be active in mercy ministry. If our congregation or gathering doesn't place an emphasis on mercy ministry (serving the poor, the suffering, the burdened, the unfortunate, etc.), we may want to seek out another congregation or a group of individuals in our denomination who share our passion for serving "the least of these." We could serve at a community organization like a food pantry, soup kitchen, second-hand store or shelter. If God's love and compassion for us compels us to do it, we just have to. If our love and compassion are overflowing, we will find a way to express it. There are others like us out there in the church. There is a faithful remnant, and Christ will be present among us. Together, we can joyfully exhaust ourselves in loving service.

It is important to share a brief word about where children fit in all this. While it may not be easy for children to live according to His will, once we teach them, the overwhelming majority will find it to be an exciting and much more meaningful life than the norm. We can help them to develop a lifestyle without all the trapping of materialism and consumerism, and where they aren't unnecessarily identified as weird, different, religious fanatics, "holier than thou," or better than anyone else. In the context of current trends in the lives of young people, they can be taught how to witness, regardless of the ethics, morals, and values of our culture, and come across without appearing to be judgmental, critical, blaming, or self-righteous. We can teach them how to witness and serve in ways that show grace, compassion, patience, gentleness, and understanding.

Chapter 13

Content with Mediocrity

What's needed to get the church back on track? We need to stop the decline and turn things around. We need to help the church reclaim its identity and mission. These were the issues about which I meditated and prayed when I thought about writing. Quickly, however, the focus shifted. The church was not going to reverse the decline, turn itself around, and get back on track.

The church has become insignificant and irrelevant. It no longer bubbles over with vitality, energy, and enthusiasm. We don't offer people much for them to get excited about, that is, a means to express their joy about being forgiven and assured of eternal life. We no longer surrender all and commit ourselves to Christ, and His mission to be a light to the nations. With the exception of a few points of light in the vast expanse of the universe, the light to the nations is flickering and about to go out. The story of the church isn't going to end well.

Nobody Listens to Me Anymore

For me, the process of addressing these issues was enlightening at first, then exhilarating, and finally, the passage to a life of discipleship. The first crossroads is deciding whether or not taking some of the limited time graciously given to an old man to address the issue is worth it. If it is not going to make any difference, if it is not going to do any good, if it is not going to change anything, then why take the time to write? Is this just an exercise in futility? Is this just a waste of time?

The church has come full circle - from insignificance to the center of it all, then back to insignificance, and now irrelevance. It began with twelve disciples, eleven of whom chose the path of martyrdom rather than deny the One in whom they believed - their resurrected Lord. Three hundred years later, it was recognized by Emperor Constantine as the official religion of the Roman Empire, and by 800 A.D., it was positioned such that the supremacy of papal authority over secular authority was established when Pope Leo crowned Charlemagne emperor of the Holy Roman Empire. The operative paradigm at that time was that God's authority flowed to the church, which yielded some of that authority to the emperor.

The church was riding high and retained a position of prominence even through two major divisions. In 1054, the Catholic Church split into the Eastern Orthodox Church and the Roman Catholic Church. Then, the Reformation began in 1517 and resulted in a division between the Roman Catholic Church and protestant churches. Through it all, and right up until just a relatively few years ago, the church occupied a prominent place in society. Now, it has quickly been relegated to the back burner as a second rate institution. The church has squandered a window of opportunity that lasted almost 2,000 years. The period in which life changed slowly ended when the pace of change began to pick up in the 1500's and 1600's, shifted into third gear in the 1700's and 1800's, and went into overdrive during the 1900's. We have now moved into a period of supersonic change and are approaching warp speed. The church has been left behind.

The daily life for common folk, throughout history, involved more than its fair share of suffering and misery. The frequent occurrence of sickness, disease, miscarriages, and mothers dying during childbirth, together with war, famine, and the occasional plague was a way of life. The church was their anchor through all of this. The priest and bishop were a beacon of hope in the midst of what was often terrible darkness. Even the immorality and greed of the ecclesiastical authorities was not enough to break the bond with those who looked to them for the assurance that God was still there, and that He cared about their daily struggle to eke out an existence in the most difficult of circumstances.

Trusting in the Lord, they struggled to survive. The magnificent cathedrals that towered over towns and cities reassured them visually that they were in the presence of an awesome, almighty God, who reigned over all. Their presence gave them encouragement. Every morning, the towering steeples greeted them and served as a beacon of hope, at least enough to get them through the day. In the evening, the steeples gave the hope needed to survive nights haunted by sickness, grief, sadness, and heartbreak.

The time when the magnificent cathedrals meant everything has become a distant memory. They are now the places tourists seek, astonished by their architecture, amazed by the engineering skills needed to build them, and overcome by the beauty of the ornate exteriors and exquisite interiors. The very best was put into every detail of these magnificent structures. The skills of designers, foremen, artists, craftsmen, and laborers were the gifts and offerings of their very selves to our Lord. It was a way for them to connect with the sacred and the holy they yearned for in the midst of their daily struggles. They were a part of all the church meant and stood for. While tourists come from afar and marvel at their magnificence, to those who live in their shadows, their spiritual significance is greatly diminished. On Sunday, they are almost empty, an apt metaphor for the irrelevance of the church in the lives of so many.

While the daily grind isn't nearly as difficult as it used to be, many still look to the church, hoping to find a beacon of hope to guide us in the midst of the issues we face today. What we find is little more than a community, which, with a few exceptions, lives its life much like most, in pursuit of the good life. Today, the church doesn't inspire hope and promise. It is not a magnificent structure built by the individual lives of dedicated people who are committed to being God's vehicles for loving, helping, and serving the needs of those who are suffering, forgotten, and living on the margins of society.

At present, we have many churches, but very little influence. If all of the churches in every city and town, would come alive, the world around us would figure out why there's a buzz. They would come to understand that it is because we're excited about Jesus and the forgiveness and salvation that are ours in Him, through His death on the cross as the substitutionary sacrifice for our sins. They would figure out that our thanks and our joy get translated into a life of self-denial and service. If we were really different, they would see it. They would figure it out.

In truth, there aren't many church folk interested in the lifestyle of a disciple. We retreated behind the walls of our church, where we have our comfort zone. We have our following, and have backed ourselves into a corner where we will not find the poor and needy, the suffering, the abandoned, and the destitute. Earlier in my ministry I fervently hoped and prayed that folks would become more compassionate and caring. I prayed that the millions who would be reached by Gospel and served in Jesus name would be blessed, as would the disciples who were serving.

Waiting for lives and congregations to change is an exercise in futility. Through the use of "holy smoke and mirrors," the church continues to deceive us by teaching and perpetuating a mistaken and misleading understanding of discipleship. The church has lost its soul, and it won't be getting it back. We've divested ourselves of our most valued asset: Christ, who came not to be served but to serve, and show compassion for the lost, the last, the least, and the lonely. We are captive to the role of accumulating our share of the American Dream. We have an inflated sense of our own importance and influence. We have a glowing, robust, positive, rosy, and optimistic narrative about ourselves that is sustained by our self-reinforcing echo-chamber.

There is a desperate need for all of us to do some serious soul searching within the framework of our own beliefs. When someone we know is in the last stages of dying from cancer, we pray for a miracle, while always adding, "Nevertheless, not my will, but yours, be done" (Luke 22:42). This is our prayer for a church that has accommodated itself to the culture, redefined discipleship, compromised Christianity, and in the process, has lost its soul.

Our indifference in a world where millions and millions are crying out in anguish and despair is a stumbling block to those we are trying to reach with the Gospel. Why in the world would we expect anyone to be influenced by anything we have to say? It is only by the amazing grace of God, working through the power of the Holy Spirit, that others are led to believe in Jesus as their Savior. The follow-up is then compromised by a demonstration of commitment whose strength can be described the way my father-in-law described his aunt's chicken soup: "She must have just let chicken run past the pot."

Why should anybody listen to us? We complain and lament that we get no respect. Why should we? What we have to say about ethics, morals, and values lacks the credibility given by a proven track record of sacrificial compassion for the marginalized, the poor, the abandoned, and the unfortunate. Thankfully, people come to faith in spite of us, through the power of the Holy Spirit working through the Gospel. Thankfully, it doesn't depend on what they see in terms of the difference that the forgiveness and eternal life, given to us through Jesus death and resurrection, makes in our lives.

We have put the cart before the horse. We tell people about Jesus and pontificate about ethics, morals, and values, while our lives do not plow and prepare the soil for planting the awesome message of the Gospel. Truth be told, we have even chosen to ride the wrong horse. We have the audacity to try to get people to listen to us. We are viewed by our culture as pathetic, self-righteous whiners. We will continue on down the road of insignificance and irrelevance. We have already been marginalized. The respect, integrity, and moral authority we once had is gone. We are not much more than one of those roadside tourist attractions that reconstruct life on the frontier in the old west. The window of opportunity has been squandered. Time has passed us by.

Now, it is time to be honest and recognize that we continue to stay the course by choice. Our hard and stubborn hearts have refused to consider a paradigm change. The very least we can do is be honest and fess up. What does that kind of honesty sound like? "Forgive us for peddling a fake and, therefore, dangerous Christianity, one where the elements of what it means to be a disciple are included on a selective basis. Forgive us for retaining the elements that folks are interested in, like forgiveness, comfort, and encouragement, while leaving out the elements that caution us about the pitfalls of participating in the pursuit of the American Dream."

Squandered Potential

Earlier I described what it is like when our child wanders away in a store, and we can't find him. It's more than panic. It's sheer terror. We scream, "Where's my child? Has anyone seen my child?" We panic and feel a sense of terror that is almost unbearable! "Please God, help me find my child." This experience and these feelings convey exactly my feelings about the church. "Where's my Church? I've lost my church!" Coming to the awareness that our church has gotten lost is sheer terror. Now we understand what that terror is about. It finally sinks in that the church began to work at cross-purposes with its own mission and is no longer what it was called to be.

God must be feeling the same way. He has abundantly blessed us beyond measure and asked us to carry on with His work in the world. His church is, at once, His second greatest triumph (Jesus resurrection is the first), as well as His greatest disappointment. At this point, I can't imagine any jolt that will shake the church out of its mediocrity and lethargy and put the brakes on its downward spiral.

Paul explained his tireless, dedicated service as a minister of Christ this way.
"Christ died for all", he explains "that those who live," that is believers, who share in Christ's death and resurrection, "should no longer live for themselves but for him who died for them and was raised again" (II Corinthians 5:14,15). [. . .] That explains why Paul sometimes appeared to be so fanatical in his ministry. He was compelled, not by law, but by love, Christ's love, to live every minute of his existence for him who in his place died and was raised.[88]

What is needed in our witness is self-sacrifice, self-denial, and concern for the poor, destitute, and disenfranchised, reminiscent of the "orders" of the Roman Catholic Church, who took vows of poverty, chastity, and obedience. With a life of discipleship, consistent with II Corinthians 5:13-15 as our calling card, at least a few will join us. We are looking for a truthful, honest, and forthright community where people really do "walk the walk."

The church lost its soul a while back. Will adopting my views on these issues make much of a difference in the effectiveness of our witness? At this point, the number that will go through a transformation will be nowhere near enough to make a difference. However, even if what we do will only be minimally effective, it is the God-honoring life. We need to be giving witness to the Gospel of Jesus Christ, and showing our love for Him by loving our neighbor.

Today, the primary teaching needing reformation is our lack of dedication and commitment. "Faith active in love is all that matters" (Galatians 5:6). We live in a whole new and wonderful world in which we graciously receive spiritual and material blessings in abundance from our Heavenly Father. We have more than those who lived before us could have ever imagined. Concurrently, we also have the potential in terms of time and treasure to help others more than ever. This opportunity has been squandered.

Discipleship has been redefined, Christianity has been compromised, and the church has lost its soul. Any hope of getting it back is no more than a pipe dream. A pipe dream is a fanciful, unlikely outcome, an unattainable hope, and an illusion. That's just the way it is as far as the church getting back its soul.

The Fellowship of the Fallen

We need to get down from our moral soap boxes and start living transformed lives of loving service. Unless we are out there every day serving the "least of these" (Matthew 25:40), we have abandoned our calling. Our current way of life only serves to tarnish and discredit the clarity, power, comfort and peace of the Gospel. We aren't interested in going down the path where self-denial, sacrifice, and service are the order of the day.

Most of our lives are cheap imitations of the real deal. We don't live lives that reflect the fullness of joy about what it means to be forgiven. We don't live lives that reflect how much forgiveness means us. We take it for granted. We act like we're entitled to it. What comes to mind was an evening drive on a state highway in Utah at the end of Interstate 70. We were the only car for miles. As we came through a pass and began coming down the mountain, the lights from the town of Delta shone brightly from 20 miles away. The night was crystal clear. It was awesome. This shining city on a hill that we call the church had its moments; it was awesome. Now, it has grown dim. The sparkling lights of its everyday heroes of faith now illuminate only a few homes. The Christmas and Easter messages from the Pope get a little coverage. The beauty of the few who are our better angels is breathtaking, as it is expressed in deep and sincere concern for the poor.

We remember the special sparkle of Mother Theresa, the twinkling of a Rick Warren, Desmond Tutu, Martin Luther King Jr., and a host of faithful Christians. Disciples, lay leaders, pastors, nuns, priests, and missionaries serving tirelessly and faithfully, most in anonymity, are today's twinkling lights. Their passion is to love others as Christ has loved them, on Calvary's cross, by serving them and giving His all for them. I give thanks to the Lord for the blessings these folks are to me. They give me a glimpse of what disciples look like. I thank God for those amazing brothers and sisters in the flock who serve faithfully like little Mother Teresas and are an inspiration and witness to me. These are the twinkling lights we see in the vast expanse of darkness of the night. Through them, the Spirit will lead a few to join us.

The world is full of those who are living in pain and misery and can't find relief from their suffering. What makes it so sad is that Christians are missing so many opportunities to serve and be a reflection of God's love to those in need all around us. These people are crying out to us. We can help, but we don't. We can bring relief to the suffering, but we aren't. The suffering and the heartbroken can be comforted. The forgotten can be visited and the abandoned can be found. However, because of our inaction, there are millions out there who are falling by the wayside. This is what hurts. If only we were more committed servants, more like the Good Samaritan, there would be so much less pain, suffering, and misery in the world. So many would experience relief, regain some sense of dignity, and find at least a little bit of hope.

Much of the Christian Church in the U.S. is afflicted with an inflated sense of its own importance. This book is a wake-up call from a friend who also drank the Kool-Aid and didn't realize it. Perhaps there will be a growing chorus of prophetic voices calling the church to repentance and renewed commitment to lives of sacrificial service. Perhaps the church can begin to find its way back and reclaim the fullness of what it means for all of us to be disciples. Wait a minute! Smack me down! Don't let me get my hopes up! It's not going to happen.

If we hope to have an impact on the world and reverse the current trend of decline, then we need a huge majority of Christians in all denominations to be active in giving an inspiring witness. This just isn't going to happen. I cannot foresee any circumstances in which there will be a great burst of energy in the church. It does not seem, to me, that we will begin to approach the critical mass needed to compel the world around us to sit-up and take notice and ask why we live the way we do. What I hope for, at best, is for some in the church to see the light and resume teaching and living what it means to be a disciple. Knowing the power of the Holy Spirit working through the Word, I have no doubt that, at least a few individuals and groups, and maybe even a few congregations will discover the fullness of joy and peace that comes from living as disciples.

Why Write At All?

Why write this narrative at all, if the church has lost its soul, and its future is not positive, hopeful or bright? Why write something about the church that is so negative and depressing? First, to give a wake-up call to the few who will be blessed to discover the fullness of joy and peace that accompany a life of sacrifice and service, a way of life that follows the assurances of grace and forgiveness in Christ.

Second, because of our flawed and negative witness as disciples, those who do not know our Savior are not being inspired and influenced to believe. While the outlook for the future is not rosy, every soul is precious. Our Lord died for each of them. Individual Christians, and small groups of believers still need to be called to live out what it means to be faithful disciples, and lead as many to Christ as they can.

Third, it is my intent to speak a word of encouragement to frustrated and discouraged preachers who have not understood a critical issue in the discussion of why the church and their congregations aren't winning more souls for Christ. Making us aware that teaching a compromised, distorted version of discipleship gives us a framework that helps us make sense out of what has been happening in the church. We realize we did the best we could with the understanding we had and can stop being so hard on ourselves. We are able to forgive ourselves, even as our heavenly Father has already forgiven us, and feel the weight of any sense of failure, inadequacy, or despair being lifted.

Finally, while I applaud those who go to church growth conferences, look to share best practices, and learn the models for congregational and denominational renewal that are being developed, they need to be aware that their good-faith efforts are built upon a flawed paradigm, and encouraged to reflect on, reconsider, modify and refocus their efforts and their models.

Now, we're ready to guide and mentor others who are on the same journey we have taken. We pray that they, too, can discover the overwhelming joy and liberating freedom that comes with assuming the mantle of a disciple. Since not much is going to change, folks who are ready to give their all to grow the church need to go into it with their eyes open. Those who have already given their all, for many years, need to know that they were doing their best, without realizing how the church was undermining and sabotaging its own efforts.

Why write at all? The Lord is still calling all of us. We all remember hearing the passages where Jesus called his disciples.

Passing along the Sea of Galilee, he saw Simon, and Andrew the brother of Simon casting net into the sea, for they were fishermen. And Jesus said to them, "Follow me and I will make you fishers of men." And immediately they left their nets and followed him. And going on a little farther, he saw James the son of Zebedee and John his brother, who were in their boats mending the nets. And immediately he called them, and they left their father Zebedee in the boat with the hired servants and followed him (Mark 1:16-20).

"He went out again beside the sea, and all the crowd was coming to him, and he was teaching them. And as he passed by, he saw Levi the son of Alphaeus sitting at the tax booth, and he said to him, 'Follow me.' And he rose and followed him" (Mark 2:13, 14).

We hear these accounts and we are inspired and moved by how they left all and followed.

My prayer is that, after reading these narratives again and hearing the call with a whole new meaning, that we have a whole new appreciation for what happened. I vividly remember worship in my home congregation, Ashburn Lutheran, on the southwest side of Chicago. Through the faithful preaching and teaching of R.J. Lillie, the Holy Spirit touched my heart and brought me to faith in our Lord. We sang "Hark! The Voice of Jesus Crying, 'Who will go and work today? Fields are white and harvests waiting, Who will bear the sheaves away?' [...] Who will answer gladly saying, 'Here am I, send me, send me.'"[89] I heard the call, came, and moved by the Holy Spirit, was ready to follow.

At that time, I didn't understand the fullness of what I was being called to do. I didn't grasp that I was being called to a life of total commitment and surrender in the same way I do now. I just knew I was being called to serve faithfully. Then, through a flawed, yet well-meaning and well-intentioned church body and nurtured with an incomplete and compromised version of discipleship, I was led by the Spirit to discover and fully understand the fullness of joy that comes along with a life of self-denial and sacrifice, in service to our Lord. Now, I hear the call differently. Now, it means so much more. Our call to discipleship is the same as the call of Jesus to His first disciples. Now, with the Spirit's strength, we can respond affirmatively with a full awareness of that to which we are being called.

The church has lost its soul, but we still have a calling. We, as individual Christians, can continue the work started so many years ago. I pray fervently and daily for the Spirit's guidance and strength, while continuing to move forward with a life characterized by self-denial and service, where I will "act justly, [. . .] love mercy, and walk humbly" (Micah 6:8, NIV). I am ecstatic about living the rest of my life as Jesus' disciple. I've been trying to follow that path through many days of celebration, many days of struggle, huge disappointments, and much heartache, and have not been disappointed.

We don't know what lies ahead. We can't see beyond the next curve in the road. We can't change the world, but we can be a reflection of God's love as we reach out and touch "the least of these" (Matthew 25:40) every day. Traveling that road will make all the difference in the world to those we serve, and to us, as we find joy, blessing, and peace beyond measure.

End Notes

[1] Barbara K. Nevers, "Not a Christian Nation," *Milwaukee Journal Sentinel,* December 11, 2016, 3J.

[2] James A. Haught, "Where is Religion Headed in the U.S.?" *Milwaukee Journal Sentinel*, December 18, 2016, 2J.

[3] David Shribman, "America's Fabric Tested Again," *Milwaukee Journal Sentinel*, March 19, 2017, 8D.

[4] Heather Choate Davis and Leann Luchinger, *SOLA!* (Los Angeles: Icktank Press, 2017), 43.

[5] Ibid., 26, 27.

[6] Francis Fitzgerald, *The Evangelicals*, (New York: Simon and Schuster, 2017), 276.

[7] Roosevelt Gray Jr., "Reaching Out to the Unchurched," *Multiplying Ministries*, South Wisconsin District – LCMS, 10.

[8] Shribman, "America's Fabric Tested Again," 8D.

[9] Susanna Schrobsdorff, "My life as a 'None" and other tales from the ranks of the unaffiliated and agnostic," *Time*, September 26, 2016, 63.

[10] Fitzgerald, *The Evangelicals*, 611.

[11] Joe Isenhower, "Reversing LCMS membership decline," *Lutheran Witness Reporter*, March 2017, 2.

[12] Heath Curtis, "Where Have All The Christians Gone?" *The Lutheran Witness, November* 2017, 6.

[13] "It's Time to Plant," *Lutheran Witness Reporter, Lutheran – Supplement*, March 2018, 1.

[14] Curtis, "Where Have All The Christians Gone?" 6.

[15] Fitzgerald, *The Evangelicals*, 614.

[16] John Burns, *Lift Up Your Heart*, (Notre Dame, Indiana: Ave Maria Press, 2016), 118.

[17] Curtis, "Where Have All The Christians Gone?" 8.

[18] Philip Chard, "Real followers of Christ act with compassion," *Milwaukee Journal Sentinel*, December 24, 2017, 5E.

[19] Fitzgerald, *The Evangelicals*, 276.

[20] Sarah Bakewell, *At The Existentialist Café* (New York: Other Press), 2012, 198.

[21] George Bernard Shaw, *The Devil's Disciple*, Act 2, 1901.

[22] John H. Kieschnick, *The Best is Yet to Come: 7 Doors of Spiritual Growth (Friendswood, TX: Baxter Press*, 2006, 56.

[23] Roland Bainton, *Here I Stand: A Life of Martin Luther (*New York: Abingdon Press, 1976, 178-179).

[24] Edward W. Desmond, "A Pencil in the Hand of God," *Time*, December 4, 1989, 11.

[25] Josep Shimek, "Reflected in the Saints among Us," *Milwaukee Journal Sentinel*, October 26, 2003, 4J.

[26] Brian Kolodiejchuk, ed., *Come Be My Light* (New York: Image Doubleday, 2007) 105, 110, 111.

[27] Shaw, *The Devil's Disciple*, Act 2.

[28] Tim Ditloff, ed., *The Ultimate Fix: Living an abundant life by focusing on the characteristics and image of God* (2017), 12.

[29] Ibid., 39.

[30] Ibid., 50.

[31] Ibid., 56.

[32] Ibid., 61.

[33] Matthew Harrison, *Theology for Mercy*, Lutheran Church – Missouri Synod, 2017, 4-6.

[34] Eugene Peterson, *A Long Obedience In The Same Direction* (Inter Varsity Press: Long Grove, Illinois, 2000), 50, 120.

[35] Kolodiejchuk, ed., *Come Be My Light*, 292, 338.

[36] Ibid., 97.

[37] Ibid., 96.

[38] Timothy H. Maschke, *Called to be Holy in the World* (Eugene, Oregon: Wipf and Stock, 2016), 32.

[39] Ibid., 43.

[40] Ibid., 157, 158.

[41] Ibid., 236.

[42] Ibid., 241.

[43] Ibid., 269.

[44] Ibid., 292.

[45] Ibid., 311.

[46] Ibid., 333.

[47] Kolodiejchuk, ed., *Come Be My Light*, 98.

[4848] Jae Yang and Paul Trap, "Most Americans Live Paycheck-To-Paycheck," *USA TODAY*, August 25, 2017, B1.

[49] Michael Learner, *The Left Hand of God* (San Francisco: Harper, 2006), 341.

[50] Bill Clinton, "The Case for Optimism," *Time*, October 1, 2012, 38.

[51] Proctor, Bernadette D., Jessica L. Semega and Melissa Kollar. 2016. U.S. Census Bureau, Current Population Reports, P60-256. "Income and Poverty in the United States: 2015." U.S. Government Printing Office, Washington, D.C. **https://.census.gov/content/dam/Census/library/publications/2016/demo/p60-256.pdf**. Accessed September 25, 2016, 12-14, 17-19.

[52] Grant Mc Govern, "A 'me' Society," *Milwaukee Journal Sentinel*, September 19, 2016, 9A.

[53] David J. Valleskey, *Second Corinthians* (St. Louis: Concordia Publishing House, 1992), 135.

[54] Ibid., 134.

[55] Ibid., 136.

[56] Ibid., 132.

[57] Fitzgerald, *The Evangelicals*, 40.

[58] Kieschnick, *The Best Is Yet to Come,* 182, 184.

[59] Stephen H. Cohen, *"Tzedakkah* – Charity," Portals of Prayer, (St. Louis: Concordia Publishing House, 2017), December 19.

[60] Julia Lieblich, "U.S. bishops Call on Catholics to Change their Everyday Lives," *Milwaukee Journal Sentinel*, November 18, 1998, 8A.

[61] Kieschnick, *The Best is Yet to Come*, 185.

[62] Ibid., 185, 194.

[63] Ditloff, ed., *The Ultimate Fix*, 65.

[64] Francis D'Emillo, (AP), "Pope on Epiphany: Don't value money most," *Milwaukee Journal Sentinel*, January 7, 2018, 2A.

[65] C.S. Lewis, *Mere Christianity Gift Edition* (New York: Harper Collins, 2001) 116, 117.

[66] Fitzgerald, *The Evangelicals*, 278, 279. (or 278-279)

[67] Burns, *Lift Up Your Heart*, 52, 53.

[68] Kieschnick, *The Best is Yet to Come*, 150, 151.
[69] Jackie Parker, "Preparing Pastors for Today's World," *Concordia Seminary (Magazine)*, Winter 2017, 8.
[70] Davis and Luchinger, *SOLA!*, 19.
[71] Ibid., 19.
[72] Maschke, *Called to be Holy in the World*, 225.
[73] *Piers Morgan Tonight,* CNN, December 22, 2011.
[74] Dietrich Bohnoeffer, *The Cost of Discipleship* (New York: The Macmillen Company, 1961), 31.
[75] Bonhoeffer, *The Cost of Discipleship*, 117.
[76] Burns, *Lift Up Your Heart*, 28.
[77] Ibid., 4.
[78] Blaise J Cuptich, "Pope Francis – A powerful witness," *Time*, May 1-8, 2017, 67.
[79] Eugene Peterson, *A Long Obedience in the Same Direction*, 89.
[80] Fitzgerald, *The Evangelicals*, 547.
[81] Ibid., 549.
[82] Ibid., 551.
[83] Ibid., 566.
[84] Maschke, *Called to be Holy in the World*, 274.
[85] Ibid., 296.
[86] Michael. J. D'augelli, "The God Squad," *Time*, July 3, 2017, 4.
[87] Elizabeth Dias, "The God Squad," *Time*, June 19, 2018, 36-42.
[88] Valleskey, *Second Corinthians*, 88.
[89] "Hark! The Voice of Jesus Crying," *The Lutheran Hymnal* (St. Louis: Concordia Publishing House), Hymn 496.

CPSIA information can be obtained
at www.ICGtesting.com
Printed in the USA
BVHW040156210819
556404BV00015B/269/P

9 781091 481534